£10.00
6/05

AC1FE

TWINS
FROM CONCEPTION TO FIVE YEARS

D1344054

BLACKPOOL AND THE FYLDE COLLEGE

3 8049 00081 806 5

7)

TWINS

FROM CONCEPTION TO FIVE YEARS

AVERIL CLEGG & ANNE WOOLLETT

FOREWORD BY JUDI LINNEY,
PRESIDENT OF THE TWINS AND MULTIPLE BIRTHS ASSOCIATION

FRANCES LINCOLN

Frances Lincoln Limited
4 Torriano Mews
Torriano Avenue
London NW5 2RZ

Twins: From Conception to Five Years
Revised edition copyright © Frances Lincoln 1998
Text copyright © Averil Clegg and Anne Woollett 1983, 1998
Photographs copyright © Nancy Durrell McKenna 1983

First published in Great Britain by Century Publishing Co. Ltd 1983
First Frances Lincoln edition: 1998

All rights reserved. No part of this publication may be reproduced,
stored in a retrieval system, or transmitted, in any form, or by any
means, electronic, mechanical, photocopying, recording or otherwise
without either prior permission in writing from the publisher or
licence permitting restricted copying. In the United Kingdom such
licences are issued by the Copyright Licensing Agency, 90 Tottenham
Court Road, London W1P 9HE

British Library Cataloguing in Publication data
A catalogue record for this book is available from the British Library.

ISBN 0 7112 1282 1

Set in Bembo
Printed in Hong Kong

3 5 7 9 8 6 4

CONTENTS

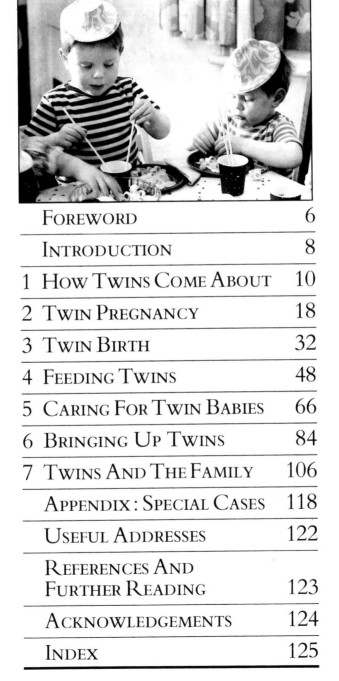

FOREWORD

Twins have always generated a great deal of interest and emotion; in the past they were even a source of myth and superstition. Nowadays, twins are seen as an enriching and exciting experience for their parents, although many feel apprehensive at first about coping with two babies at once.

Parents of twins constantly stress their need for information and understanding to help them through the crucial first years of their twins' lives, a need that has not been met by baby care manuals to date. Drawing together the latest research, the many new ideas that have emerged in the last few years and the personal experiences of over forty twin families, Averil Clegg and Anne Woollett help fill this gap, providing admirably clear and much-needed information on twin birth, care and development.

The management of twins both antenatally and after the birth forms only a small part of the training of health care professionals. *Twins* will act as an invaluable source of ideas and information for those who have responsibility for the health and welfare of twins and will help them understand the problems of parents and their twin children.

Emphasizing the pleasures of having twin children, the authors describe the many changes and special experiences of twins as they grow mentally, physically and socially. The importance of individuality is rightly stressed, and this book helps to reassure parents who may be worried by their twins' different rates of development, while helping them to understand and enjoy the separate personality of each twin.

Watching and guiding your twins from childhood to independence brings untold rewards to parents. This book, with its evocative photographs and sensitively drawn illustrations, captures the emotions and relationships between parents and children and provides an engrossing record of the experience of having twins.

Mrs Judi Linney,
SRN, SCM, HV, HEd,
President of the
Twins and Multiple Births Association

INTRODUCTION

Twins are special and very exciting. The possibility of having twins passes through the minds of most pregnant women, but it usually comes as a surprise when it actually happens. Parents generally greet the news with mixed reactions; they are pleased and often delighted, but they also have many questions. Some are about immediate things, such as how long the pregnancy will last and what to expect at the birth. Other questions look to the future, and are about how to take care of two children. Parents who already have one or more children ask questions about how to ensure that all of their children get along together and are treated fairly. Many parents look for babycare books to answer their questions and for advice, but very few of these have a great deal to say about twins. It seems either that twins and their mothers are rarely thought of as special or it is assumed that advice and information about one baby can be readily extended to two. But parents say repeatedly that this isn't the case and that their questions go unanswered.

In this book we offer information and suggestions for parents of twins to consider. By encouraging parents to plan ahead and think about how they want to bring up their twins we hope they will feel confident about themselves as parents and will enjoy their twins to the full. Some things about twins are quite different from single born children. They are more likely to be born early, and often develop a closeness and mutual understanding, so they find great fun in one another's company and in their twinness. Parents may feel very privileged to have twins – they soon notice the extra interest and attention they attract as a pair, so parents need to think more carefully about their individuality and whether or not to treat their twins alike. Other things are a question of 'more' rather than 'different'. Looking after two babies and then two children takes longer than looking after one, especially two of the same age. With twins there are two routines to be worked out and fitted together. All parents of new babies get tired, but parents of twins can become exhausted, and so feel in need of extra help and understanding. Grandparents, friends and neighbours can often see that there is more to be done with twins and are pleased to get involved. It is quite clear, too, that fathers can have a really important part to play. Their help can ensure that both parents can make the most of their time with their children.

Although our book is mainly addressed to parents, we have also written it for those who are close to families of twins – whether as relatives or professionals involved in their care – so that they can understand better the need for encouragement and support.

Parents of triplets and quads are another group who can use this book, since there are many aspects of twin care that apply equally to triplets and quads. Once it is discovered that you are having more than one baby, great care is taken of you during your pregnancy and birth. Triplets and quads are tiny babies likely to need special care, so that you probably want to think carefully about how to feed them, look after them and bring them up. Many of the issues we raise and the suggestions we offer for two can be extended to three or more babies.

What we say in this book comes from a mixture of sources. As professional psychologists and as women interested in women's health, we have drawn on a range of medical and psychological ideas about having children and bringing them up. In particular we have drawn on more than two hundred interviews with families with young twins.

The question arose about how to refer, without confusion, to each twin child, and to other children in the family. In order to make the text easy to read, we decided to call all twins 'she' and all other children 'he'. We also talk about single or single born children. This is not a reference to their parents' marital status, nor does it mean that they are 'only' children, but simply indicates that they are born one at a time, to distinguish them from twins.

Averil Clegg and Anne Woollett
April 1983

1 HOW TWINS COME ABOUT

Women sometimes wonder during their pregnancy whether they are going to have twins—even now a few do go undiagnosed until birth. 'How did I come to have twins?' 'I'm carrying very high, does that mean twins?' 'They say I'm big for dates, could that be twins?' 'I thought you only had twins if they ran in your family.' 'My grandmother had twins. Do you think that means I'll have them?' 'How can there be two inside you? There just doesn't seem to be room!' 'What makes twins so alike?' 'How do twins come about?' The list of questions seems endless. Mothers wonder if they are having twins immediately after birth, when, having delivered one baby, they are amazed at their still very large stomachs!

For the majority of mothers, questions like these are quickly dismissed or forgotten. But for a number of you, they do become a reality, and your experience of pregnancy, childbirth and childcare are all greatly altered by having twins.

HOW COMMON ARE TWINS?

The ratio of twin births to single births varies considerably in different countries, although the incidence of identical twins is about the same. Identical (uniovular) twins occur in about 3 to every 1000 pregnancies which go to term throughout the world. Non-identical (binovular or fraternal) twins have a recognized hereditary basis and vary between the highest incidence which is recorded in the Yoruba tribe of Nigeria as 46 in 1000 (the rate is about 25 per 1000 in Nigeria as a whole), to Japan where the incidence of fraternal twinning is about 1 in 1000 (giving a total twinning incidence in Japan of 4 per 1000 – 1 non-

identical and 3 identical). The incidence in Britain is between 11 and 12 per 1000, a figure which is similar to America and other European countries.

Conceiving one baby

During each menstrual cycle a woman's ovaries produce an egg. Under the control of the female hormones (oestrogen and progesterone) a number of eggs (ova) begin to develop each cycle. One grows faster than the others, is pushed to the surface of the ovary and is released. This is called ovulation. Once one egg has been released the hormones prevent the growth and release of any more eggs.

The egg then travels down the Fallopian tube where fertilization takes place. One sperm breaks through the egg's outer wall, and the genetic material (chromosomes) from the mother and the father is combined. Once fertilization takes place no more sperm can get through the egg's outer wall.

The chromosomes begin to divide, first into two cells, then into four, eight and so on. This cell division continues as the fertilized egg, called the zygote, moves down the Fallopian tube and into the uterus where it embeds itself in the endometrium or lining of the uterus.

The zygote continues to divide rapidly and different groups of cells develop to do different jobs. Some develop into the embryo, others become the placenta, and the amniotic sac. The placenta acts as an organ of exchange between mother and developing baby, providing nourishment and oxygen and removing waste products. The baby develops in a pool of fluid (the amniotic fluid), enclosed by a bag or sac with two layers, the inner amnion and the outer chorion.

Identical twins

The conception and early development of twins is similar to that of single babies, but there are a number of important differences according to the type of twin.

An identical twin pregnancy starts in exactly the same way as a single pregnancy; a single egg is released and is fertilized by a single sperm. The resulting zygote begins to divide but then, for reasons which no one yet understands, the cells divide an extra time and split apart, producing two separate but almost identical zygotes. This split often happens in the Fallopian tube, but the division may take place once the zygote is embedded in the endometrium. Identical twins usually share one placenta and one chorion but have separate amnions. If the zygote divides in the Fallopian tube, the twins are more likely to develop separate placentae, chorions and amnions. Occasionally they have a single amnion as well as a single chorion. Identical twins are sometimes called monozygotic or uniovular (deriving from one ovum or egg).

The incidence of identical twins does not appear to have any measurable hereditary tendency, since the accidental splitting of one fertilized egg apparently occurs completely at random.

Non-identical twins

Non-identical or fraternal twins occur when the mother produces two separate eggs during the same cycle, both of which are fertilized by different sperm and travel separately into the uterus. Non-identical twins always have separate placentae, amnions and chorions, although sometimes they may embed themselves so closely together in the endometrium that their placentae fuse. They are called binovular or dizygotic, meaning that they develop from two fertilized eggs or zygotes.

Some women frequently produce more than one egg at each menstrual cycle, and are therefore more likely to give birth to non-identical twins. This tendency may run in families, and may come through either your mother's or your father's side of the family, and often through both. Your partner, however, has no influence on whether or not you conceive more than one baby at a time.

Age is also a factor; women in their late thirties are more likely to produce at least two eggs during each cycle, raising the likelihood of non-identical twins from a pregnancy at that age. Women who already have three or more children have the same tendency. So if you are over 35 and have already had several children, you are more likely to have twins.

Mothers over the age of 35 are among those more likely to have a tendency to produce two eggs (ova) during one menstrual cycle and so give birth to non-identical twins, like these two-year-old twin girls.

Another group of women who are more likely to have non-identical twins are those who have been given ovulation-inducing drugs for the treatment of sub-fertility. Clomid increases the twinning rate and very rarely can produce higher multiples. Pergonal and similar drugs have

TWIN CONCEPTION

Conception of one baby occurs when one egg is released from a woman's ovary at ovulation. Shortly afterwards it is fertilized in the Fallopian tube by a single sperm (right). After ejaculation, the sperm travels up through the vagina and the uterus and into the Fallopian tube. The fertilized egg (now called the zygote) divides into two, then four, then eight and so on. It continues to divide as it moves down the uterus. Here it embeds itself in the endometrium (lining of the uterus), establishing a single pregnancy.

Identical twin conception occurs when one egg is fertilized as in a single conception, but later splits into two zygotes. These move down the Fallopian tube separately and embed in different places in the endometrium (below left) developing into identical twin embryos with separate placentae. Sometimes the zygote does not divide until it has actually embedded in the endometrium (below right), thus developing into identical twin embryos sharing one placenta.

Non-identical or fraternal twin conception occurs when a woman releases two separate eggs during one menstrual cycle. Both the eggs are then fertilized separately by two individual sperm. These develop with completely separate placentae (opposite, below left). If the two zygotes embed close together, their placentae may fuse (bottom right). Fused placentae can also occur with identical twins.

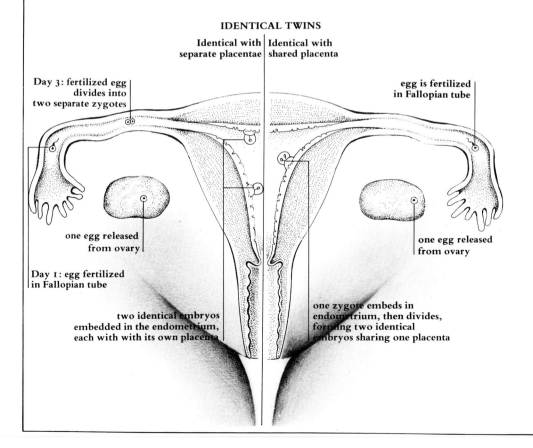

IDENTICAL TWINS

| Identical with separate placentae | Identical with shared placenta |

Day 3: fertilized egg divides into two separate zygotes

egg is fertilized in Fallopian tube

one egg released from ovary

one egg released from ovary

Day 1: egg fertilized in Fallopian tube

two identical embryos embedded in the endometrium, each with with its own placenta

one zygote embeds in endometrium, then divides, forming two identical embryos sharing one placenta

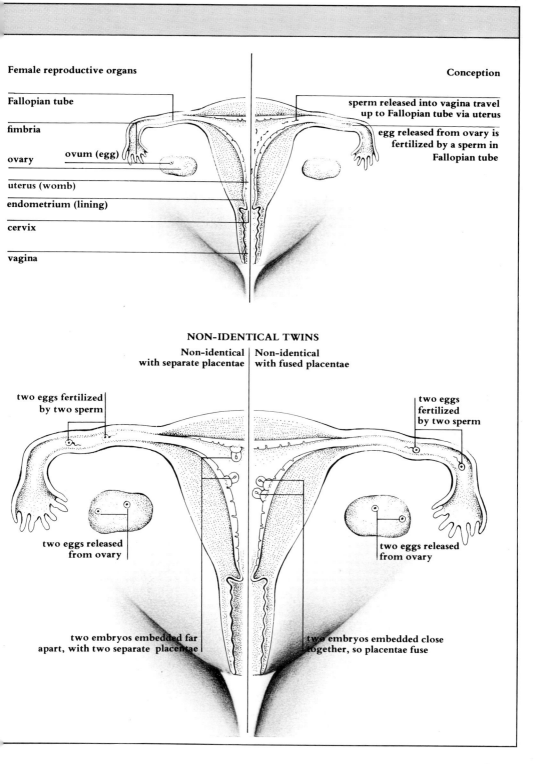

Female reproductive organs

Fallopian tube

fimbria

ovary   ovum (egg)

uterus (womb)

endometrium (lining)

cervix

vagina

Conception

sperm released into vagina travel
up to Fallopian tube via uterus

egg released from ovary is
fertilized by a sperm in
Fallopian tube

NON-IDENTICAL TWINS

Non-identical | Non-identical
with separate placentae | with fused placentae

two eggs fertilized
by two sperm

two eggs
fertilized
by two sperm

two eggs released
from ovary

two eggs released
from ovary

two embryos embedded far
apart, with two separate placentae

two embryos embedded close
together, so placentae fuse

TWIN FORMATION

Identical twins

Identical twins are formed by the accidental splitting of a single fertilized egg, so that two babies develop from one egg and one sperm. Twins that develop from this early cell division are known as identical, monozygotic (from mono = one; zygote = fertilized egg), or uniovular (from uni = one; ovum = egg).

Non-identical twins

Non-identical twins develop from the fertilization of two eggs by two sperm. Twins that are formed this way are known as non-identical, fraternal, dizygotic (from di = two; zygote = fertilized egg), or binovular (from bi = two; ovum = egg).

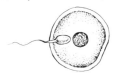

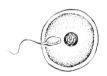

Girl and boy twins

Identical girl twins

Non-identical girl twins

Identical boy twins

Non-identical boy twins

helped many women to ovulate and bear children, but when first introduced their effects were a bit haphazard, so that twins and higher multiple births were not uncommon. Monitoring the drugs' effects is now much improved, but there is still a chance of twins, occasionally triplets or even higher multiples.

DISTINGUISHING IDENTICAL AND NON-IDENTICAL TWINS

If your twins are of different sexes they are non-identical since identical twins are always of the same sex. However, if they are of the same sex, it can be difficult to tell whether they are identical or not. Complex blood tests may be carried out to determine their zygosity (whether they developed from separate fertilized eggs or one egg which then split). Once the babies begin to grow and develop, non-identical twins of the same sex are usually no more alike than any pair of sisters or brothers. In contrast, identical twins always look alike, with the same features, hair and eye colouring, and it can be difficult to tell them apart unless you know them very well indeed.

THE IMPLICATIONS OF ZYGOSITY

Twins' zygosity may influence how they are treated both within and outside the family as they grow up. If your twins are a boy and a girl or if they do not look very much alike, you may find that you and their friends and family treat them as individuals. If you find it difficult to tell your twins apart you may treat them more like one another. But there are all sorts of other factors which affect how you feel about and behave towards your twins: whether they are small and premature babies; whether they are quiet and placid; whether they are noisy and demanding of your attention; or whether they sleep and feed well. We talk about some of these things in later chapters.

2 TWIN PREGNANCY

FINDING OUT
THAT IT'S TWINS

Some women suspect for themselves that they are having twins; there may be a history of twins in their families. Being large for dates, lots of very vigorous movement and rapid early weight gain are all signs that may alert you or the antenatal staff to the possibility of twins. On the other hand you may experience these signs but have no idea that you are having twins. The news comes right out of the blue during your routine antenatal care or sometimes even not until delivery.

The early stages of twin pregnancy can be quite uncomfortable. Women often say that they feel very nauseous, disoriented, tired and moody, and sometimes more so than for a single pregnancy. Because they feel this way, they may wonder whether there is something wrong with their pregnancy. If you feel like this, learning that you're expecting twins can come as a relief, since it will reassure you that there is nothing wrong. It's just that the extra changes in your body are causing unusually strong symptoms.

DETECTING
TWINS

Twin pregnancies can be detected in a number of ways. One method is to listen for two heartbeats. This can be done using an ear trumpet or, if available, a sonic aid or a fetal heart monitor, which use microphones placed against your abdomen to amplify the sound of your babies' hearts. The larger machines blip visibly and print out a paper trace of the heartbeats. Another way of detecting twins is by palpation, or gently feeling the surface of your abdomen. The medical staff may be able to feel two sets of limbs, two heads and two bottoms, and later you may feel these for yourself. But it is possible to miss twins by these methods when one lies right behind the other; the baby in front obscures the one behind. Perhaps the most frequent and most reliable way of detecting twins is by ultrasound scanning.

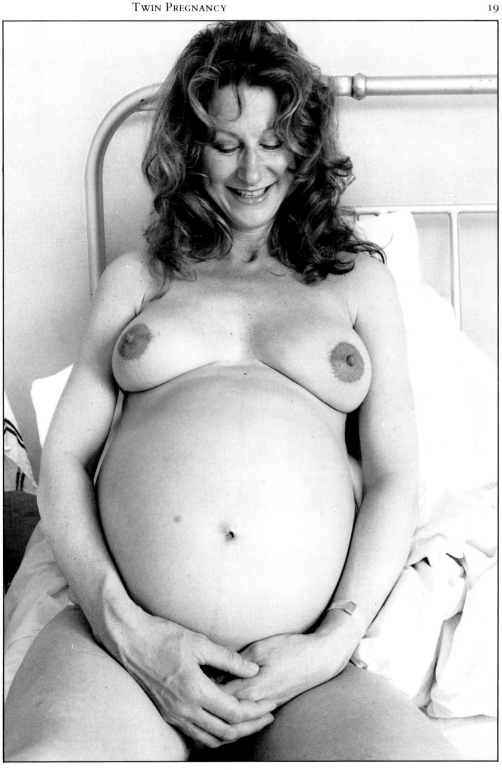

In some hospitals ultrasound is a routine part of natenatal care, given to all women. Elsewhere it may only be used when there is a special indication such as when your uterus is considered to be large for your dates. Routine scans are usually given between twelve and sixteen weeks, so you will probably have your twins confirmed by sixteen weeks. If scans are not given routinely, you may be asked to have one later in pregnancy, when it is even easier to detect twins in this way.

THE SPECIAL NATURE OF TWIN PREGNANCY

Twin and single pregnancies are similar in many respects. Even the most normal of pregnancies can have its discomforts, owing to the weight of the growing baby and the demands made on the woman's body. Fatigue, backache, constipation, varicose veins and haemorrhoids (piles) are frequent and normal complaints of pregnancy which all women find a nuisance. Although many women find pregnancy a time when they feel very well, others find it makes them feel fat, unglamorous and uncomfortable, and twin pregnancies do add to the discomfort. The gap between the image of the glowing pregnancy and the reality may seem more acute for you, especially as you may be bigger at six months than the average woman bearing one child is at term.

However, the excitement of looking forward to twins and feeling special often compensates for the discomforts. Your partner, family and friends may share this excitement and this may make it easier for them to recognize your special needs and come forward with offers of help. Pregnancy can be a time when you and your partner have lots to share. If you are a single mother you may approach the changes in your life in other ways. Try to build up friendships with people who can support and help you.

ANTENATAL CARE

Pregnancy with a single baby usually lasts on average about 40 weeks and women increase their weight by approximately 12.5kg (28 lb), though this may vary a great deal from woman to woman. Twin pregnancies are much more likely to be shorter than single pregnancies, but despite this you will probably gain more weight than you would have with one baby. These are reasons why you will have greater care taken of you during your pregnancy.

You may be asked to attend antenatal clinics more frequently than other mothers, particularly towards the end of your pregnancy. If ultrasound scans are not available in your hospital, you may have to go elsewhere for them, which can increase your visits. You may be able to organize shared care between your family doctor, community midwife and the hospital clinic. Shared care can be more personal; you get to know your doctor or your midwife and you may have less travelling; but what is available varies according to where you live. Check with your family doctor or local health centre if you are not sure.

Twin births are unpredictable so you are advised to book into a hospital for the birth, even if you had hoped for a home delivery. The

TWIN DEVELOPMENT

MOST IDENTICALS

shared placenta

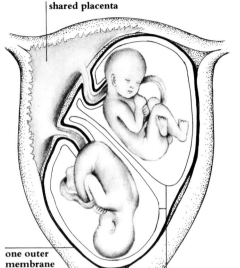

one outer
membrane
(chorion)

separate inner
membranes
(amnions)

SOME IDENTICALS AND NON-IDENTICALS

separate amnions   separate placenta

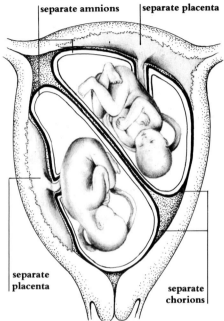

separate
placenta

separate
chorions

SOME IDENTICALS AND NON-IDENTICALS

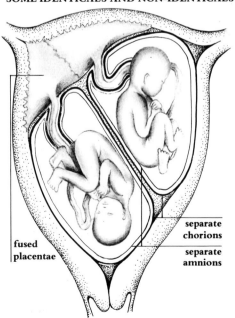

separate
chorions

separate
amnions

fused
placentae

A fetus is protected inside the uterus by a bag of fluid which has two membranes, the outer chorion and inner amnion, and is connected by the umbilical cord to the placenta. The placenta links the babies to their mother during pregnancy, providing nourishment and oxygen and removing their waste products. Identical twins (above) often have separate amnions surrounded by a single chorion and share one placenta. Most non-identical twins have separate placentae, chorions and amnions (above right). Some identicals and non-identicals have separate amnions and chorions and separate placentae (right) which may fuse if close together.

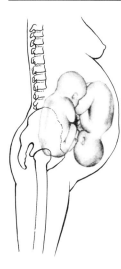

Above: Very occasionally a second twin is not discovered until delivery. Usually this happens because her presence is shielded in this way behind the first baby, so only one heartbeat may be heard and one set of fetal limbs felt.

larger maternity units are equipped to deal with possible emergencies; in addition they can care for your babies more adequately if they are born prematurely.

The progress of your pregnancy is followed carefully at the antenatal clinic. The staff pay particular attention to your weight, blood pressure and any signs which indicate that you are retaining a lot of fluid. Ultrasound scans check your twins' growth and their positions. You are advised about diet and health care in pregnancy and about the arrangements for your delivery. Take advantage of offers by the antenatal staff of tours of the labour and postnatal wards and the Special Care Baby Unit. Your visits to the clinic also provide you with an opportunity to ask the questions you have about being pregnant, even if you already have a child. You live with your pregnancy every day so you know whether there seems to be anything unusual about it. For instance, it is normal to vomit occasionally in early pregnancy, but frequently vomiting, every day for a week or so, should be brought to the attention of the clinic staff. For your own sake, as well as your babies', let them know if there is anything particularly worrying you. Although the antenatal staff may be busy, they will do their best to answer your questions and put your mind at rest. They do not want you to go away worried or to miss appointments.

You may like to make a list of your questions in advance and ask the doctor or midwife to leave time to discuss them with you. You may feel more confident if you take someone along to the clinic with you. If there is anything you do not understand ask the staff to explain in less technical language. There may not be ready answers to some of your questions, because it is not easy to predict the future for an individual. It is worth remembering that a twin pregnancy is an exciting event for the medical staff as well; they will take a special interest in you and will spend extra time on your antenatal care.

COMPLAINTS IN TWIN PREGNANCY

The extra weight you carry and the demands twins make on your body mean there are often minor complaints in your pregnancy which are not serious and rarely need medical care. It helps to know they are not much different from the normal complaints of a single pregnancy.

In early pregnancy

The main complaints are fatigue, nausea and vomiting. If you feel sick try to avoid fatty foods, eat little and often and try to get someone else to do the cooking if you cannot face it yourself. It is quite a good idea to have a piece of plain toast or a biscuit before you get up since an empty stomach does seem to make the symptoms worse. Glucose is a good antidote to nausea, so you may want to try one of the commercial glucose drinks, glucose sweets or tablets, or try any sweet food that appeals, such as toast and honey. If you vomit, make sure you drink plenty of fluid. If vomiting becomes severe, tell your doctor at once. Nausea and vomiting usually pass after three or four months. Many women are overcome by waves of fatigue during pregnancy, whether

TWIN PRESENTATION

1 Both twins cephalic or head-first. About half of all twins present in this way, which causes least problems. at the birth.

2 One twin head-first, one breech. Almost as many twins present in this way. The head-first twin is usually born first.

3 Both twins breech. This is less usual; many of these twins are delivered safely by Caesarean section.

4 One twin head-first, one transverse (crosswise). Very few twins present this way. The transverse twin is sometimes turned before birth, or may be delivered by Caesarean section.

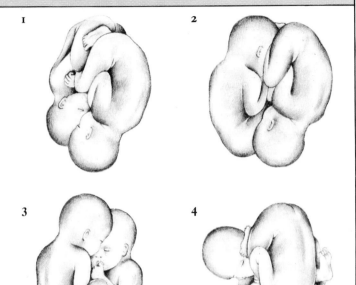

they are expecting twins or not. Try to rest as much as you can; if you feel the need to go to bed early, do so. Once you know you are having twins, people can be sympathetic about how tired you feel.

In later pregnancy   Most of the complaints of later pregnancy come about because of your size. You can expect to be unusually large, because you are not only carrying two babies, but also two lots of amniotic fluid and often two placentae as well. Quite how big you become depends on the size of your babies and how many weeks pregnant you are when you go into labor. A few women gain half as much again of their pre-pregnancy weight when they have twins. If you go to 37 weeks or more, you can expect to be very large—you may outgrow your maternity clothes and will certainly find simple everyday chores like doing the washing-up more difficult than usual. If you can, try to see the funny side of it, and remember that however large you become you gradually get your figure back again after your babies are born.

Your uterus becomes heavy and stretched, increasing the pressure on your stomach, groin, chest, ribs, back, legs and heels. This can lead to fatigue, breathlessness, difficulties in sleeping, walking, eating and climbing stairs. Take things very slowly, rest often and pay particular attention to your posture; to avoid straining your back always bend your knees if you need to pick something up from the floor, and sit with your feet up as much as possible. If you have a lot of heartburn eat little and often and drink milk to settle the acidity. Your doctor may prescribe a suitable antacid medicine. Relaxation and gentle exercise help to avoid stiffness and discomfort such as backache (see pages 26–27). If you have varicose veins try to avoid sitting with your legs crossed, and if you have uncomfortable haemorrhoids try to eat more fibre. If necessary ask your doctor to prescribe a suitable ointment.

COMPLICATIONS IN TWIN PREGNANCY

Some of the minor complaints of pregnancy can occasionally become serious and there are some clinical complications which are relatively common in twin pregnancies. Many of these conditions require treatment in hospital, so you may spend a few days or more on the antenatal ward during your pregnancy. The following chart describes some of the complaints and how they are treated.

Complication	Treatment you may receive in hospital
severe vomiting	intravenous fluids; sedatives to relax the stomach.
slow growth of twins	rest; frequent scans; check by fetal heart monitoring; or advice to rest a lot at home.
anaemia (deficiency in red blood cells)	iron and folic acid.
fluid retention/gross swelling of body and/or limbs (oedema)	rest; possibly diuretics (to remove fluid).
bleeding	before 28 weeks, may be threatened miscarriage. Possibly initially treated by bed rest. After 28 weeks may indicate problems with placenta. Treatment initially may include bed rest plus fetal monitoring; fetal distress may indicate induction (see below). In both cases ultrasound scans used to locate placenta.
diabetes	sometimes starts in pregnancy; more common with family history of diabetes; glucose tolerance test at 28 weeks and possibly blood sugar levels tested repeatedly (sugar series); insulin prescribed.
hydramnios (excessive fluid in the amniotic sac)	rest.
toxaemia or raised blood pressure, also known as pre-eclampsia and eclampsia	rest; drugs if necessary to reduce blood pressure, induction if it is very bad or persistent.
threatened premature labour	rest; possibly drug treatment; may end in premature birth. (See below).
ruptured or leaking membranes (or amniotic sac)	in mid pregnancy rest to forestall further leakage; in later pregnancy induction if labour does not start spontaneously by about 36 weeks.
failing placenta or fetal distress	Close observation followed by induction or Caesarean section depending on the severity of the problem.

THE IMPORTANCE OF RECOGNIZING PREMATURE LABOUR

A single pregnancy usually lasts for 40 weeks, but only a small proportion of twin pregnancies go on this long. It is normal for a twin pregnancy to be shorter; some women deliver much earlier, and 36 to 37 weeks is average. Indeed, 38 weeks is often considered as term for twins, and your doctor may suggest induction if you go on longer than this.

Because labour can start so early, it is important for you to recognize the signs. If you think you may be in labour, do not hesitate to get in touch with your doctor, midwife or your hospital labour ward. Don't worry about asking for advice or seeming silly; the staff will not mind false alarms, especially with twins.

Delaying labour

If you go into labour very early in your pregnancy and even if your membranes are broken, the hospital may try to delay or arrest labour by putting you on an intravenous drip containing a drug to relax the muscles of the uterus. Once the contractions cease, you are taken off the drip, given the drug in tablet form and you have to rest in hospital. You may be kept in hospital for some weeks and monitored daily for any re-occurrence of early labour.

Symptoms	What to look for and what to do
Ruptured membranes	If water pours from your vagina, your membranes have broken and labour may have started. *Don't wait to call your doctor, but go to hospital immediately.*
Leaking	Leaking may happen because of pressure on your bladder (which is a normal and temporary nuisance in pregnancy) or your membranes may be leaking. *Call your doctor or go to hospital.*
Contractions	These occur throughout pregnancy as tightenings of the uterus (Braxton-Hicks contractions). However if these tightenings are recurring on average once in every 15 minutes, you may be in labour. *Call your doctor or go to hospital.*
Backache	Contractions sometimes start as persistent backache. If the backache starts to come and go rhythmically, and perhaps at the same time to extend round to the front, then *call your doctor or go to hospital.*
Period pains	Early contractions can feel very like the pains of menstruation. *Call your doctor or go to hospital.*
Bleeding	Labour often starts with a small loss of blood-stained jelly-like material, called a 'show'. This may indicate that the cervix is beginning to open. *Call your doctor or go to hospital.*

PREPARATION FOR TWIN BIRTH

Pregnancy can be a particularly anxious time if you are expecting twins and you may start to watch for signs of labour with mixed feelings. Your increasing discomfort may make you look forward to going into labour, but you know that if labour starts too early your babies may be small and sickly. With twins it is a good idea to be ready to go to hospital for treatment or delivery at any time after 28 weeks. This means having your bag packed, informing your partner, family and friends, and arranging for your other children to be cared for. Almost all parents talk about being on tenterhooks during the last few weeks of pregnancy while they wait for signs of labour. They wonder about whether they will recognize the signs, whether the ambulance will arrive in time, and whether the message will get through to the father at work. It is comforting to know that almost all parents go through this, whether or not they are expecting twins.

SELF-HELP DURING PREGNANCY

Most women experience swings in their feelings as they go through pregnancy. Whether their pregnancies are planned and a source of great joy, or whether they come as a complete, and perhaps unwelcome shock, they can feel happy some days and low at other times. Your pregnancy may be associated with lots of other changes in your life, especially if it is your first. For example, it may mean that you stop working outside the home, so you lose the interest of your work and the company of your workmates.

Rest and relaxation

The extra demands on your body made by twins mean that you are advised to take special care of yourself. The most common advice is to rest as much as possible, and if you can, it is really worthwhile doing so. Try to sit with your feet up and support yourself with cushions. You may find it more comfortable to lie down while you read or watch television. If you are not someone who finds it easy to relax, you could join a relaxation class. Your local hospital or the National Childbirth Trust may be able to tell you how to find a class that suits you. These often teach you gentle exercises, and special breathing techniques to help you through labour and childbirth.

If you are working or have other children, there may be less opportunity to rest, and this may not seem like advice you can take up. At work you can try to put your feet up for an hour or to use the rest room. Look round for what you can cut down on if you have a lot of commitments. Spend your evenings quietly or invite people round to see you. If you've got toddlers see if you can find someone to take them off your hands for an hour or two each week. Most mothers know how tiring pregnancy can be and may be willing to help you if you explain how extra tired you feel because you are carrying twins.

Posture and exercise

If you go to antenatal or relaxation classes, you will learn ways of walking, sitting and lying that help your body cope with the extra strain. You can experiment with pillows to find ways of lying in bed that allow you to sleep as well as possible. Propping yourself up so that you are almost sitting sometimes helps you to sleep better. Exercises tone up your muscles and keep you fit. The fitter you are, the less your discomforts distress you and the better prepared you are for labour. Swimming is a good all-round exercise and is often recom-

POSITIONS FOR RELAXATION

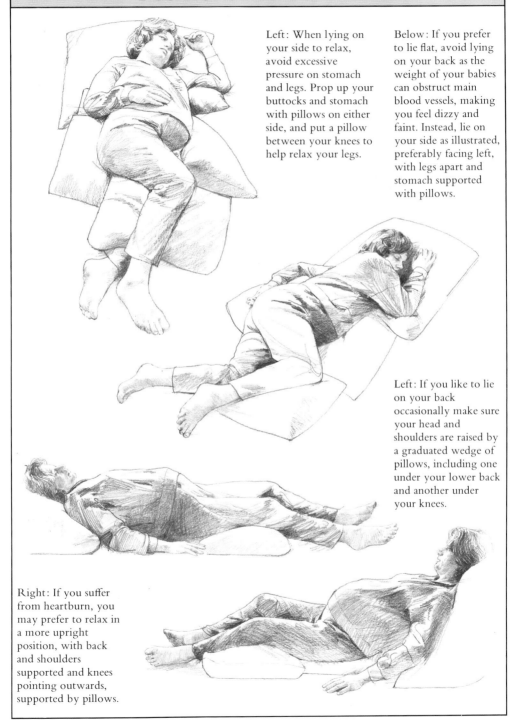

Left: When lying on your side to relax, avoid excessive pressure on stomach and legs. Prop up your buttocks and stomach with pillows on either side, and put a pillow between your knees to help relax your legs.

Below: If you prefer to lie flat, avoid lying on your back as the weight of your babies can obstruct main blood vessels, making you feel dizzy and faint. Instead, lie on your side as illustrated, preferably facing left, with legs apart and stomach supported with pillows.

Left: If you like to lie on your back occasionally make sure your head and shoulders are raised by a graduated wedge of pillows, including one under your lower back and another under your knees.

Right: If you suffer from heartburn, you may prefer to relax in a more upright position, with back and shoulders supported and knees pointing outwards, supported by pillows.

mended for pregnant women as the water helps to support your extra weight.

Diet

You are nourishing two babies as well as yourself, so your diet is important. You will feel less exhausted if you make sure you eat a well-balanced diet with plenty of proteins, calcium, fresh fruit and vegetables. A good supply of bran or other fibre helps prevent constipation. Try to avoid the fried and fatty foods which increase heartburn and nausea. If you don't feel you can eat much, try to eat little meals frequently. If you can't face cooking proper meals there's nothing wrong with convenience foods for a while, or try to persuade your partner or a friend to cook for you occasionally.

Clothes

With twins you are likely to be in maternity clothes for a long time. You will need to wear them earlier than other mothers-to-be and may not get your figure back as quickly after the birth. Choose things you feel happy in and which have plenty of room for you to expand. Maternity trousers may not be suitable after about six months, so you may prefer to invest in only one pair, using maternity dresses most of the time. Borrow clothes from friends or from your antenatal group so you get less bored with your own. It is important to wear a good supportive bra, day and night if necessary, and some women like to go to a shop where they can be properly fitted. If you are planning to breast-feed, don't wait until your babies are born, but buy front-fastening maternity bras whilst you are still pregnant.

Buying things for the babies

With two babies you'll need more of some things; extra clothes, nappies, toiletries, cots and carry cots. See if you can buy disposable nappies in bulk—it saves shopping and expense later, but does depend on storage space. You may want to buy a twin pram; write to the leading manufacturers for details of what is available so that you do not have to spend time and energy going round shops. Having twins is generally more expensive than having two single babies with an interval between each, since you cannot hand things on, but you can keep costs down by borrowing or buying second-hand equipment. Your baby clinic, antenatal clinic or Twins Club might be a good place to keep an eye open for advertisements for good quality secondhand clothes, prams and pushchairs, cots and baby baths. The twins' grandparents may be pleased to help out with large items like a twin pram or cots, washing machine or tumble dryer.

GETTING HELP
Fathers

Fathers often think that pregnant women become very engrossed in themselves and so can feel left out; they may feel more a part of what is happening if you let them listen or do things for you. Try to take your partner into your confidence so that together you can share your worries and excitement. He may be able to come to some of your antenatal check-ups and be pleased to be able to ask questions and understand what happens in the clinic. He could ask about being with you at the birth and discuss hospital rules and procedures with the medical

TWIN PRAMS AND PUSHCHAIRS

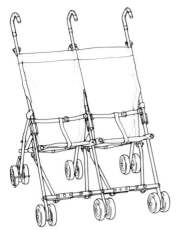

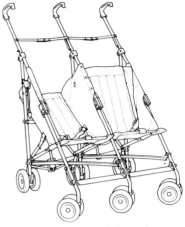

Above: The so-called 'buggy' or 'stroller' type of pushchair has revolutionized infant mobility. This is the simplest type of twin buggy, which folds completely and is relatively light to carry. Some manufacturers supply rainhoods or covers.

Above: A more sophisticated form of twin buggy with adjustable backs. These are better for younger babies who may want to sleep while out for a walk, as they allow the babies to lie in a more horizontal position.

Above: The buggy frame has been further refined by one manufacturer to accommodate a carry cot as well as an adjustable buggy seat. Both twins may fit in the carry cot while they are small and your toddler can sit in the seat. This type may also be worth considering if one of your twins is more wakeful than the other

Above: The conventional twin baby carriage, in which the babies lie end to end. If you choose this type of pram, the babies can take turns to lie facing the person who is pushing the pram giving each a chance to look at you and talk to you.

staff. (Some fathers really enjoy seeing their twins for the first time on the ultrasound screen.)

At home let your babies' father take over as many of the chores as he feels he can manage. Explain to him how difficult it can be to get things done, for instance shopping and carrying things. Point out which activities are especially difficult when you are so heavy and with which you most need help.

Housework

Decide on your own priorities; you are the best person to know what they are. If you and your partner cannot do everything because you are too tired and he is out at work all day, you may have to let your standards go as far as you can bear to. If you find it hard to relax when there is housework to be done, do those jobs that are most important to you. Try to leave the rest or persuade someone else to do them occasionally or consider getting some paid help. It does not help you or your babies if you are drained but your house is spotless. The more other people understand what is happening to you and how you feel, the more they can help.

Other people

Your own mother or mother-in-law may be prepared to help. Pregnancy and babies often help to bring mothers and daughters closer together, even if you seemed to have little in common before. Many grandparents are particularly proud when twins are on the way and are happy to help with washing, housework or looking after other children. You may need help during the day with young children so you can relax and put your feet up. Your family may be willing to run errands for you or drive you around by car, if you cannot do this for yourself. You probably enjoy your pregnancy more if you are able to get out to see people as much as you like.

However, if your family live some distance away it may be difficult for them to offer help regularly. Friends and neighbours who live close by may be a good source of help and may be better able to step in at short notice. It is always helpful to have someone sympathetic to talk over with you your many plans for and your thoughts about your babies, particularly when you're feeling a bit low. If you feel you can, do try to ask for help when you need it and to take advantage of it when it is offered.

PLANNING AHEAD

In the last few weeks before the birth, mothers expecting twins often find they have to rest, since their size makes any activity difficult. Use this time to plan ahead for the birth and for bringing your twins home afterwards. Make sure you know how to contact the hospital; give essential telephone numbers to friends, family and your partner and work out how to get the message to him or whoever is coming with you to the hospital.

If you have other children they'll need looking after, so get it arranged as early as you can with someone who realizes he or she may have to take over at a moment's notice. Make sure this person has the telephone number of the hospital and of your children's playgroup or school. It is probably a good idea to have someone else in reserve as well.

Pack your bag for the hospital well in advance, putting in extra things like books and writing paper. Most hospitals encourage fathers to be present at the birth, but you should probably check first if it is not offered. or if you want anyone else to be with you at that time. On the whole, hospitals do not allow more than one person at a time in the labour ward.

ACCEPTING
YOURSELF

One of the most important ways of making the best of your pregnancy is to accept yourself as you are and not to mind that you do not necessarily approach it the same way as everybody else. Few women go through their pregnancies like the carefully posed models in advertisements. Some women seem unconcerned by things that cause worry to others; some like to plan and organize while others prefer to take things as they come. Some seem to have pregnancies that go by the book; for others, one problem seems to lead to another. Some women are impatient to have their babies; others are more able to enjoy the experience of being pregnant. Try to concentrate on the good things about your pregnancy, especially when you may have to search around for them. They may include feeling your babies moving inside you, getting lots of extra attention from other people, excitement about becoming a mother, seeing new sides to your own or your partner's character and taking on new roles. Bear in mind that a difficult pregnancy doesn't necessarily mean that you won't have a straightforward or enjoyable labour and childbirth. Remember, too, that it is not essential to have a glowing or even a healthy pregnancy for you all to develop loving relationships with your babies.

3 TWIN BIRTH

THE STAGES OF
LABOUR

Labour and birth are always described in three stages. During pregnancy the cervix or the opening of your uterus (womb) remained tightly closed, sealed with a plug of mucus. During the first stage of labour the muscles of your uterus contract rhythmically and powerfully and these contractions (labour pains) pull open the cervix and the baby's head gradually bulges through into the vagina. When your cervix has opened or dilated to about 10cms the baby moves down the remainder of your vagina towards its opening. You are now in the second stage of labour, and you usually feel a very powerful urge to push. Normally, working with your contractions, you push your baby down the birth canal, head first, into the world. The delivery of the placenta, shortly after your baby is born, is the third stage of labour.

A twin birth follows the same course with a gap between the delivery of the first and second baby. The first stage is the same, but as there are two babies, the second stage is repeated; you go through the pushing and the delivery twice. If the twins share a placenta, both twins are born before the placenta is delivered. When each twin has her own placenta, both placentae are usually delivered after both the twins are born. Very rarely the first twin's placenta is delivered before the second twin is born, and then the second twin's placenta is delivered. Twins are often small babies, and their little heads pass relatively easily through the birth canal. Once the birth canal has stretched to allow one baby to pass through it, the second baby can pass easily. For these reasons twin labours and deliveries are seldom longer than single ones.

PRESENTATION

The way in which babies are born depends on their position in the uterus. Most single babies are delivered head first, with a small proportion delivered in the breech position (legs or bottom first). Approximately 50 per cent of all twins are both delivered head first. Almost as many twins are born one head first and one breech; usually it is the second twin who is breech. Occasionally both babies are in unusual positions. A head-first delivery is considered normal and is associated with least risk for both you and the babies.

SHARING THE DELIVERY

Labour and birth can be much more enjoyable if you have someone special, such as your partner, with you. You may be surrounded by equipment, machines and medical staff, so it helps to have someone present who concerns themselves with your needs, keeps you company, shares the experience and helps to relive it with you later.

The more complex your delivery, the greater the need for someone to explain what is happening and to help you have your wishes and needs understood. If there are no problems with the baby, the person with you may hold the first born while you concentrate on the second, or bring you news of your babies' progress if they are taken into special care. Twins can create very special opportunities for their parents to share memories later on and to appreciate the different ways they were both able to cope.

OBSTETRIC PRACTICES AND INTERVENTIONS

If you have already borne children you may recognize many similarities between your single and twin labours and births. However, with twins there are extra concerns to take into account, including how long your pregnancy has lasted, the size of your babies and the positions in which they are lying. Particular concern is felt that with either one of your twins the placenta may not continue to work well until the baby is born. This means that it may become necessary to deliver both babies early. Unfortunately, one of the most predictable things about twin births may be their unpredictability!

Because twin labours are even less predictable than single labours, you may have a highly supervised labour, and experience a number of obstetric practices and interventions that are used in childbirth. These include the induction or acceleration of labour, the monitoring of the mother and babies, and the administration of anaesthetics, and if your babies are very premature you may be given an injection to mature their lungs. Exactly which, if any, of these interventions are used depends on your progress in pregnancy and labour and on the facilities available at your hospital. Very occasionally it is decided to move you from one hospital to another where they have better facilities (transfer in utero).

Finding out in advance

Sometimes things happen very quickly at delivery, and your delivery team may be too busy to stop and explain things to you or to ask you about your preferences. It is helpful if you have seen the delivery ward and found out in advance what is available. In this way you have a better idea about what is happening. If you want to have some say about the kinds of obstetric practices or interventions you receive, it is important for you to discuss the possibilities with the medical staff while you are pregnant, and again when you first go into labour. This way you may find it easier to take an active part in the decisions of the midwives and doctors caring for you. Women sometimes say that they feel less sure about what will happen with twins and so they are not able to be very clear about how they want their deliveries to go. Sometimes they also say that because twins can be tiny they are more ready to accept the medical facilities offered to them, because they appreciate that these reduce the hazards for them and their babies. Not all twin births mean a lot of medical intervention; you do not necessarily experience many of the interventions listed. Do also remember that knowing about possible problems and how they are dealt with does not make them more likely to happen to you. However, if you understand what the possibilities are, you are better able to understand what is happening to you and why. This may help you to hold on to what is happy and good about the birth of your twins.

Induction and acceleration

Induction means the artificial onset of labour. You may be induced if you are ill, for instance with diabetes or high blood pressure (see page 24). The doctor may suggest induction if the placenta is not functioning well and your babies appear to be in distress. With twins these complications are more likely to happen, so there is a higher chance of your being induced even when your twins are still premature. Some obstetricians prefer not to let mothers of twins go to full term, even if they show no signs of spontaneous labour.

Induction may take the form of breaking the amniotic sac (artificial rupturing of the membranes or ARM), or you may be given hormones by pessary (prostaglandins) or by drip (syntocinon or oxytocin). The drip is a fine tube attached to a needle in a vein in the back of your hand. The tube leads to a bag of fluid supported by a stand at the side of the bed. Glucose (to give energy) is often introduced through the same tube. Sometimes an automatic version of the drip (the Cardiff pump) is used, which regulates the amount of hormone you are given according to the strength of your contractions.

Accelerated labour If you go into labour yourself but it is thought that you are progressing too slowly, you may be speeded up or accelerated. Again this may be by ARM or by using the drip.

An induced or accelerated labour may differ from a spontaneous labour; contractions build up more rapidly and become stronger more quickly. You may feel less able to use your breathing exercises to control and cope with your contractions and so you may be more likely to use pain relief such as epidurals (see page 41). If you have been to classes and want to use your breathing exercises, let the midwife and medical staff know early in your delivery.

Monitoring labour

In all deliveries it is important to monitor progress, and there are a wide range of techniques available. At intervals during labour, you are examined internally to measure the dilation of your cervix and descent of the head in the pelvis. The medical staff can feel the top of the baby's head by abdominal examination once it is engaged. This tells them which way the baby is facing and the position of the head as it descends into the birth canal. The frequency and to some extent the strength of your contractions can also be assessed by feeling the surface of your abdomen. Unless you have an epidural you yourself can assess the frequency and the length of your contractions and how strong they are. If you have your partner or a friend with you, they can help you do this. The babies' heart rates are a good indication of their general state and are measured frequently during labour. They can be picked up with a trumpet or fetal stethoscope and also with an electronic monitor. The monitor can print out on paper tape a record of your contractions and your babies' heartbeats. It may also amplify the sound of the heartbeats and display them as 'blips' on a small screen, so you can watch and listen to them. The information is registered through sensors (electrodes); one is attached to the first twin's head, the others are fitted across your abdomen with straps. The wires leading from you to the machine limit your ability to move and the sensors attached to your abdomen can make relaxation, massage or breathing exercises difficult. The sounds they make can have a hypnotic quality, so that some parents find themselves being fascinated by the machines. In addition, like all gadgets,

The progress of a twin labour is very often monitored by a machine similar to this one. The mother's contractions and her babies' heartbeats are being picked up by sensors attached to her abdomen. All three are registered on the simultaneous paper trace slowly unrolling from the right of the monitor.

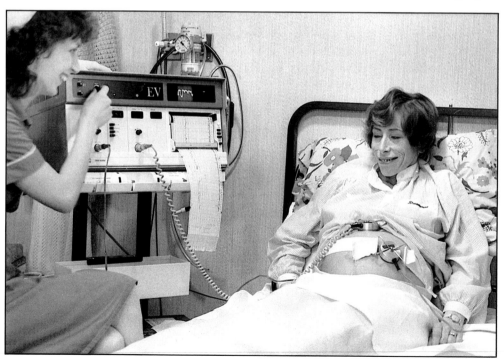

they can go wrong. It can be very alarming suddenly to see your baby's heart rate cease to register on the monitor, even though it probably only means that one of the sensors has come adrift. However, these machines can give an accurate and continuous record of each babies' state and how labour is progressing which may be particularly re-assuring if you have an epidural and cannot feel your contractions.

Episiotomy This is a small cut in the base of the vagina (perineum), usually made under local anaesthetic. An episiotomy is generally performed for a forceps, ventouse or breech delivery and when the second twin is turned internally (internal version). Sometimes an episiotomy is also performed when the medical staff consider the baby is short of oxygen, the perineum is too resistant or that it may tear. An episiotomy is stitched after delivery, also under local anaesthetic. The stitches are gradually absorbed but they can be uncomfortable for a few days after the birth.

Assisted deliveries **Forceps delivery** Forceps can be used in the second stage to help the birth of one or both of your twins in a number of situations. One is when delivery is difficult because your babies arrive in awkward positions. Forceps can help the birth of a baby presenting in a breech position. To protect the baby's head and neck, a breech delivery is done slowly; you are carefully guided about when to push, and you may find yourself waiting some minutes for your baby's head to emerge. The second twin is breech in about 36 per cent of twin births; it is much rarer for both twins to be breech. Forceps can also be used when epidural anaesthesia means that you are unsure about when or how to push; when your uterine muscles are overstretched and not working efficiently; when you are too tired to push well; or when your baby is distressed. These things happen more frequently with twins, so forceps are used more often than they are for single deliveries.

Ventouse (or vacuum) extraction Sometimes this technique is used instead of forceps. When the baby is ready to be born, a small metal cap is attached to her head and held there by suction. This is then used to help ease the baby out.

Caesarean section Caesarean section means that your baby is removed through an incision (cut or opening) in your abdomen. A Caesarean can be planned in advance (known as an elective Caesarean) if difficulties are anticipated, for instance, if the placenta is positioned between the baby and your cervix (placenta praevia), or when both twins lie in positions which are potentially risky. Alternatively, you may go into labour, but if one or other of your babies registers distress for some reason, a decision may be made to remove one or both of them by Caesarean rather than go ahead with a vaginal delivery. (This is known as a selective or emergency Caesarean.) Occasionally the first twin may be born vaginally and the second by Caesarean section.

For a Caesarean section, your abdomen is cut either vertically, or more often, horizontally along what is known as the bikini line, and your babies are lifted out one by one, followed by their placentae.

A twin birth is something for both parents to share (below), even though in this case, weakening of the mother's uterus during a previous birth has meant that an elective Caesarean is to be performed, under a general anesthetic.
The first twin emerges head first (right) while the second is breech (bottom left). Both babies are weighed (bottom right) and their overall condition checked.

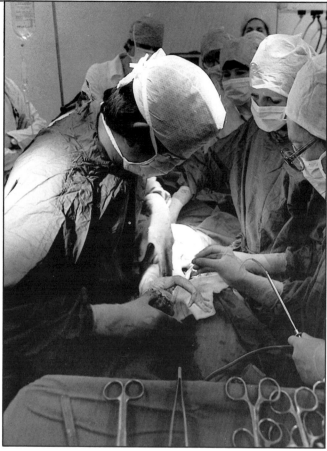

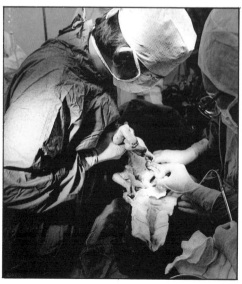

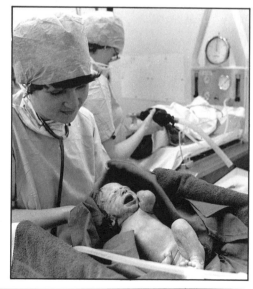

Even though the twins were born while their mother was under general anaesthetic, the babies' father is able to hold them immediately after the birth and to begin the process of getting to know them both.

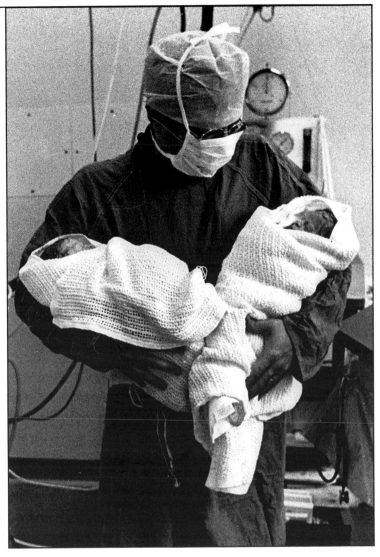

Caesareans always used to need a general anaesthetic, but it is becoming more common for them to be done using epidural anaesthesia (see page 41). This way you remain conscious throughout, but the lower part of your body is screened from view, and you do not usually feel any pain from the operation although you may be aware that things are happening. The great advantage of Caesarean by epidural anaesthetic is that you are able to see and hold your babies as soon as they are born. In addition hospitals are increasingly allowing fathers or others to stay with you during the operation.

A Caesarean section is a serious abdominal operation. You will have pain from the wound and sometimes air is trapped inside you. You may have trouble finding a comfortable breastfeeding position at first. The operation leaves you with less energy and you may tire easily in the first two weeks. You need extra help when you go home from hospital and it may be several months before you feel as well as you would like to.

The Second Twin

Concern about the second baby is the main reason for medical intervention in twin births. The first twin may be well position and be born without undue stress, but the second twin often has more difficulty.

When the first baby has been delivered your abdomen is checked to see that the baby's heart rate is normal. Her position or 'lie' is also checked. If she is lying transversely (across), your doctor gently manipulates her from the outside of your abdomen (external version) so that she comes to lie longitudinally (up or down) with either her head or her bottom first. If your baby cannot be turned from outside, she may be turned from inside (internal version). A check is made in case the umbilical cord is coming out first (prolapse of the cord) because this would mean that she is not getting a good supply of blood and hence not getting the oxygen she needs.

The aim is to have not too long an interval between the delivery of your twins; some doctors like the second baby to be born between five and fifteen minutes after the first. In order to encourage the delivery of the second baby the medical staff may break her sac of amniotic fluid. If the contractions do not start up again of their own accord shortly after the birth of your first baby, you may be given syntocinon through an intravenous drip. This is done in order to stimulate your uterus to start contracting again.

Sometimes your doctor may wish to deliver the second baby more rapidly. This can happen, for instance, if the baby becomes distressed, if there is a prolapse of the cord, if you begin to lose a large amount of blood (interpartum haemorrhage) or if the second baby is lying transversely and cannot be turned round.

When your baby's birth does have to be speeded up in this way, your delivery team are more likely to use forceps or ventouse extraction, or they may decide on a Caesarean section. If you have not already been given an epidural, a general anaesthetic may be used for some of these more complicated procedures.

Although most doctors and midwives prefer to deliver the second twin without delay, there is often enough time between the two births for the mother or the father to see and hold the first twin before the second is delivered. If your first baby is well enough and you are not given her to hold but you would like to, do ask or get your partner to ask. It can be a readily bright spot in your delivery. On the other hand, if you are feeling tired and holding the baby seems more than you can cope with, don't be afraid to say so as well. You will have lots of time to love and hold your babies later when you are feeling stronger.

THE RELIEF OF PAIN

For most women pain is an integral part of childbirth. The amount of pain different women experience varies widely; so does the amount of pain that they are able to tolerate. What feels just uncomfortable to one woman can be very painful to another. How much pain you feel able to cope with depends on your individual pain threshold, whether you are frightened or relaxed, how well prepared you are and whether you have people around you who are able to help you cope. It should not be seen as a test of your moral strength or determination.

Pain is associated with childbirth for a number of reasons. Uterine contractions stretching the cervix are the main reasons in the first stage; in the second stage pain is associated with pressure and stretching of the birth canal. Some of the procedures used by the medical team to assist delivery can be painful as well. However there are a number of ways of relieving pain during labour and birth. At your antenatal or childbirth classes you may learn relaxation and breathing for first stage contractions. Many women find these techniques helpful, and can be assisted by their partners, even if they also use other kinds of pain relief. Gas and air (entonox) and pethidine are also generally available.

Epidural anaesthesia

In some hospitals, mainly the large or teaching hospitals where there are anaesthetists trained in this technique, you may be offered or advised to have an epidural anaesthetic or a similar technique known as a caudal block. An epidural is a local anaesthetic injected to block the nerves before they join your spinal canal. It removes most sensation but particularly pain from the lower region of your body. It is usually an extremely effective anaesthetic. To be continuously effective, it needs to be topped up every three or four hours, so sometimes feelings do reappear as the anaesthetic wears off. Because you cannot feel anything most of the time you may not be able to tell when you are having a contraction, nor when you want to push in the second stage, but the medical staff can feel the contraction and tell you when to push.

An epidural is especially useful in a complicated delivery, when for instance the medical staff may wish to turn the baby to a better position or to use forceps to assist delivery. These are of course procedures which mothers prefer to undergo with the help of painkillers, so try not to be too upset if you need anaesthesia when you had hoped not to.

POSTNATAL CARE

The obstetric practices you have experienced may leave you feeling uncomfortable. If you had forceps, you probably feel bruised and sore. Stitches from tearing or from an episiotomy can be very uncomfortable, and even soluble ones take time to disappear. The scar from a Caesarean section can take a long time to heal properly and you may continue to feel it for some time when you bend or when your clothes rub it.

After a serious operation you would normally be advised to take things easily for some weeks. After a difficult birth you need rest as much as someone who has had a major operation. But it is generally assumed that you take care of your babies very soon after the birth, though you may have a few days or even weeks respite if the babies are in special care. Your babies may be looked after in the nursery until you are well enough to cope, especially at night.

In the postnatal ward you are taught to care for your breasts and, if your babies are in special care, how to express your milk. Try to make yourself comfortable. Ask the midwives if there is any extra treatment you can have to help the healing of stitches or your Caesarean wound. Heat treatment for instance can be used to relieve the pain after a forceps delivery. Take hot, salty baths and try to make yourself relax in the water. Do the exercises recommended by the hospital physiotherapists, although they may suggest you take things very gently at first, especially if you had a Caesarean. If your stitches are sore, try using an air cushion.

When you feed your babies, use pillows to cushion yourself against the pressure they exert on a Caesarean scar. It is quite usual to be uncomfortable after a complex delivery, but if the discomfort goes on for weeks, do see your doctor and make sure you tell the medical staff of any problems at your postnatal check-up.

WOMEN'S FEELINGS ABOUT THEIR BIRTHS

Giving birth to twins can leave your feelings in a jumble. Pain, shock, regret, disappointment and sadness intermingle with relief, disbelief, numbness, joy, pleasure and love. These mixed emotions may be appropriate. Your twins' birth can be the good experience you've probably hoped for, but there is a good chance that it is not. You may feel it is out of your control, as there is, unfortunately, much less opportunity for you to take advantage of some of the new attitudes to childbirth. But often parents of twins emerge from their experiences feeling quite positive; in spite of births which are all too often real ordeals, they are able to reap whatever is good from the experience. They are pleased, for instance, that fathers (mothers or friends too, but mainly fathers) are usually allowed to stay during delivery.

How you feel about your birth depends on many things. Your general approach to life influences your reactions, since different people handle things in different ways. You are affected by how you hoped and expected your delivery to be; whether your twins were expected or whether the double arrival was a surprise; how the birth went and how much pain or discomfort you feel afterwards. Then you consider your babies; you may be sad if they are poorly so you cannot hold them, but thrilled because you are quickly able to respond to them and to love them. If you had a difficult pregnancy you may be relieved that the babies are born at last. And however you feel about the birth, you may be excited at being able to hold or feed your babies afterwards.

But it is not only your body which may have suffered; your emotions may also be in a state of shock. Emotional healing is as important as physical healing after a difficult birth experience and both take time. Most mothers, whether they have twins or not, feel weepy at some point after a birth, and even fear they may never want another baby. Even if you have a long stay in hospital you may not be fully recovered physically before you go home. It may take longer still for your memories of the birth to fade. Eventually, however, you do feel more comfortable, you feel less confused by the experience of giving birth and you come to see yourself as a mother to your twins.

THE SPECIAL BABY CARE UNIT (BABY WARD)

Most hospitals have some specialized care for premature, tiny or sick infants, but the facilities vary very much between hospitals. If babies require the kind of care which is not available in one hospital they may be moved to another with more extensive facilities. Women expecting twins are sometimes shown the babies in the special care unit and told about its work during their antenatal visits. This means that if your babies go into the baby ward you are better prepared for how small they can be, what tiny babies look like, and all the equipment in the ward. If your clinic doesn't volunteer to show you round, consider asking for a visit. The staff are sympethetic when you are expecting twins, since they know that twins are often small or premature.

PREMATURE BABIES

Babies go into the baby ward for a variety of reasons; prematurity is one of them and low birth weight is another. A premature baby is one who is born before the 37th week of pregnancy; a low birth weight baby weighs less than 2500 grammes (5lb 8ozs) at birth. Twins tend to go into the baby ward for both reasons. 2450 grammes (5lb 6oz) is an average weight for twins; 'big' twins tend to be small compared with single babies. Babies also go into the baby ward because they are jaundiced, have breathing difficulties or because they are unable to keep warm. Premature babies may suffer from these conditions but not always.

Twins may be taken to the baby ward because they are small, and not necessarily because they are sickly; in fact they may be doing well for ones so little.

HOW THE UNIT WORKS

A full scale intensive care unit has three areas: very hot, warm and cool. Very small or very sick babies are kept in the hottest room, where the temperature may average 25°C (82°F). These babies are unable to feed themselves; their breathing is often poor and they find it difficult to keep warm, so they have to be helped if they are to survive. They are kept in incubators which provide the special environment for each one's needs. In the hot area in particular the babies are surrounded by a bewildering array of equipment. It is used to monitor the babies, to check that they are getting the right amount of food and oxygen and that they are keeping warm. As they grow bigger and more able to cope on their own they are taken out of their incubators, and the tubes and wires attached to them gradually removed. First they may move into a cot in the hot nursery, then into a cooler room, so moving means progress and it's a sign to look forward to.

THE APPEARANCE OF PREMATURE BABIES

Very premature babies can look quite unlike our images of beautiful babies. They are small, and their cries and their features can be startlingly different from the babies elsewhere in the hospital. They are usually thin and wrinkled and covered with fine downy hair. At first some parents can be shocked by their babies' appearance, although they quickly get used to them, and can see beauty in their ugliness. They are so tiny that their helplessness can excite tender, loving and protective feelings, and many parents grow to see only their babies' beauty. If you find your babies unattractive, try to not be too concerned; they will outgrow their funny looks as they get bigger.

LENGTH OF STAY IN THE UNIT

Parents of a twin in special care soon become familiar with the important functions of all the initially alarming tubes and wires.

Twins are quite often taken to the baby ward shortly after they are born. You are usually allowed to hold them and touch them for a while first, though this does depend on circumstances. Twins often stay in the unit for only a few hours before joining you on the postnatal ward. Their stay is just a precaution to make sure that they are well. Other babies stay for a few days but are able to return to you in time for everyone to go home together. Others stay in even longer, and you may be discharged from hospital before your babies are ready to go home.

If your babies are in the baby ward for some time, you are both

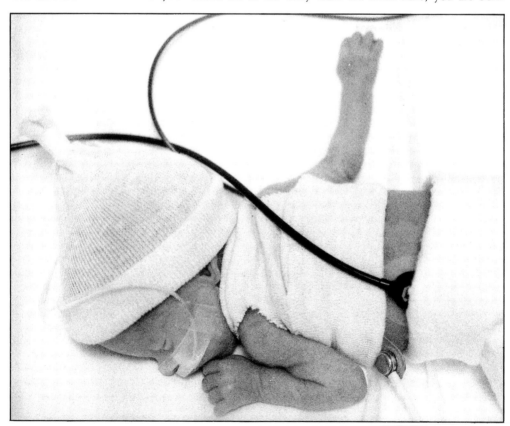

encouraged to visit them and to help with their care as much as possible. Sometimes there is a parents' room where you can rest and have refreshments, and a few units even have overnight facilities. There may be a social worker attached to the unit who can offer you advice and talk over any problems you wish to discuss.

FEEDING IN THE SPECIAL CARE UNIT

The best thing you can do for very small babies in incubators is to provide breast milk. Very tiny babies, under about 30 weeks gestation may not be able to take even breast milk at first, and may be fed special nutriment from an intravenous drip. But they will need milk when they grow bigger, and you can help your supply by expressing your milk frequently. The hospital staff will store your milk for the babies by pasteurizing and freezing it. When they no longer need to be fed with a drip, your babies will be able to take breast milk. At first they are not able to suck enough for their needs, so they are fed with a fine tube which is passed through their noses into their stomachs. Milk is put through the tube with a syringe. Later they will take milk from a bottle with a special soft teat, and eventually as they get bigger and stronger you are able to start putting them to the breast.

While they are building up their ability to suck they may be fed partly with a bottle and partly by tube, or partly at the breast and partly by bottle. Expressing your milk may seem a time-consuming and lonely chore, but for tiny premature babies breast milk really is the best food. It is easy to digest and it gives them protection from infection. There are generally breast pumps available in the unit and electric ones are becoming more common. Electric pumps are the easiest to use and are especially useful if you are going to express milk for some time.

If you leave hospital before your twins, you can express your milk at home, storing it in the hospital's sterilized bottles and keeping it in your refrigerator until your next visit. Sometimes the hospital or one of the birth organizations can lend you or hire you an electric breast pump.

If you decide not to breastfeed your babies, they may be given some-one else's expressed milk to start with from the hospital's milk bank. They move on to ordinary formula milk and normal teats when they are able to cope with them.

OTHER PRACTICAL CARE

How much you can do for your babies depends on their size, state and the amount of medical treatment they are receiving. If they are very small, expressing your breast milk may be the only kind of practical help you can give your babies in the special care unit, because the nurses see to everything else. You can probably comfort your babies and perhaps help them to thrive by being there, by talking to them and by touching and stroking them through the portholes in the incubator. We do not know how and in what ways babies can respond to their sur-roundings at this early stage, but doing these things may help them, and getting to know them may comfort you as well.

Unless they are very premature or sick, you are often encouraged to change and wash your babies within a few days of birth. Once they are out of the incubator, you are shown how to bath them. Try to ensure that this happens when their father can be present, since this is a good time for him to begin to care for them as well. If you are nervous about looking after such tiny babies, the nurses are there to help.

It is always very hot in the hot nursery and you are asked to wear a gown over your clothes to protect the babies from infection. So wear thin clothes, and be prepared to stay for only a short time if you find the heat oppressive.

Feelings About The Special Care Unit

Parents express lots of different feelings about the special care unit. With all the tubes and the wires, it may be a bit alarming and seem like an uninviting place to get to know your babies. But your relief that they are alive and being well looked after may help you overcome your doubts about their surroundings. You could perhaps try to make the most of this time in other ways. While your twins are in the unit, you have a chance to recover your strength, especially after a difficult delivery. It gives you time to adjust to being the mother of small and needy babies and, if necessary, to finish preparing for their homecoming. This can be very useful when your twins were unexpected, or arrived well ahead of schedule, and you were taken into hospital at short notice. Most separations are short and parents are usually able to spend as much time as they wish with their babies in the unit, so they do not generally think, in the long run, that their feelings about their babies are affected.

Most parents find the staff of the special care baby unit understanding and helpful. If your twins are very small and sickly, you may quite naturally be anxious about how well they are doing. At such a time your unhappiness, frustration and anger can all get mixed together, and being parents of sick, tiny babies is a painful experience. The behaviour of the baby unit staff may seem to you very cool and unconcerned. You may be tempted to direct your anxiety and your anger towards them even though this is not the best way to help yourself. In the first uncertain days, the staff often share parents' anguish and concern, but they have learned that the only way they can function well in their emotionally demanding job is by controlling their feelings. Otherwise it would be easy for them to become overwhelmed by working all the time with sick babies and anxious parents.

If you want to talk about your feelings, and many parents feel that they do, speak to your family or to friends who are willing to listen. If the baby unit has a social worker, he or she may be able to help by encouraging you to talk freely about how you feel. Other parents of twins who have been through similar experiences may understand and support you in ways few other people can. Your nearest Twins Club may be able to put you in touch with parents in your area, if you feel that this would help. (See page 124.)

KEEPING IN TOUCH WITH YOUR BABIES

Some mothers go home first, leaving their babies in the special care baby unit. Hospitals generally encourage parents to visit as much as they can because they recognize how much it can help both parents and babies. Visiting times are often fairly unrestricted for parents, but older brothers and sisters and other relatives may not be allowed in or they may be confined to an observation area.

If you live at some distance from the hospital you may find it physically tiring and very expensive to visit your babies as often as you would like. You may have older children to care for and you may be concerned about their feelings as well as about your twins. You have been separated from one another so you can use the time before your twins come home to be with your older children and to re-establish your relationship with them.

If you feel that you cannot visit your twins as often as you would like, their father may be pleased to go anyway because he will be missing them too. The hospital may allow other members of your family into the unit if you explain how difficult it is for you yourself to visit.

You probably miss your babies and wish you had them with you, and you may worry about them if there is still concern for their well-being. Never hesitate to ring the baby unit day or night to ask how they are. Concerned parents are loving parents, and are never considered a nuisance by the staff.

WHEN THE TWINS COME HOME

Even when one baby is ready to come home before the other, many hospitals prefer to keep them together in the nursery until the smaller or sicklier baby is also ready. Most parents of twins agree with this policy since they sometimes fear that they will become more attached to the baby who has been at home longer and then find it difficult to adjust to caring for two babies simultaneously.

When the time comes for you to take your twins home, some hospitals invite mothers to stay for 24 hours or even longer. This is to give you an opportunity to take over full care of your babies while still having the support of the hospital staff should you feel you really need it. This gives you some experience with your babies and boosts your confidence, hopefully making it easier for you to manage well when you have them all to yourself at home.

Arriving home with two babies is exciting – and sometimes a little frightening. Try to arrange for someone to be there to help. Take a deep breath and try to relax. It's going to be hard work, but you'll cope.

4 FEEDING TWINS

DECIDING HOW
TO FEED TWINS

Parents of single babies have lots of advice about feeding them. They get information from their own mothers, sisters, friends, from the antenatal clinic, books, television and so on, and they may have watched other mothers feeding by breast or bottle, so they have an idea of how it is done. When it comes to thinking about how to feed twins there is less advice available, and little of it comes from a direct knowledge of parents' own experience of feeding their twins.

BREASTFEEDING
OR
BOTTLEFEEDING

Some women feel very clear about how they want to feed their babies. You may know that you want to feed your twins by breast or bottle – perhaps because you have fed other babies that way. Or you may be less certain. You may take it for granted that you'll try to breastfeed, at least in the beginning, and see how it goes. Women approach the issue of how to feed their babies in different ways, and their decisions are based on a whole range of factors; nutritional, health, and personal. When you discover that you're having twins, you may want to think again about how to feed. You may have felt fairly confident about breastfeeding or bottlefeeding one baby, but feeding two raises some different questions. Small babies are often slow feeders and need to be fed frequently – sometimes as often as every two to three hours each at first. Twins may take time to get into a regular pattern of feeding, and even when they do you cannot guarantee that their routines coincide. Even if they are good, strong feeders you still probably spend more time feeding in the early months than doing anything else. Since you are going to spend much of your time feeding your twins, it's important

that you feed in a way that gives you as much satisfaction and pleasure as possible. Your needs and feelings need to be considered as well as your babies'. Some of the advantages and disadvantages of breast-feeding and bottlefeeding twins are given in the chart.

BREAST	BOTTLE
Gives protection from infection.	Offers no protection against infection.
Easily digestible.	Can be slightly more difficult to digest at first.
No-one else can feed unless you express your milk.	Your partner, family and friends can all help with feeds.
Requires no preparation apart from looking after your breasts.	Bottles have to be sterilized.
May need persistence to establish milk supply if babies are small and slow feeders.	Milk supply is always guaranteed even if babies are slow feeders.
Difficult to tell how much babies are getting without test weighing.	Easy to see exactly how much each baby is taking.
You can feed both babies simultaneously if you wish.	Difficult to feed simultaneously unless babies are propped up or chairs.
You need to devote time to eating and resting well to produce enough milk.	Being tired and busy does not affect milk supply.
Not possible to feed two babies discreetly in public.	Babies can be fed anywhere, and by anyone.
Physically very tiring.	Tiring, but others can help you.
Eating well costs a little more than your normal diet.	Cost of formula milk for two babies can mount up.
Requires planning if you want to wean both babies from breast to bottle to go back to work.	No physical adjustment needed for you or babies if you are going back to work.

Feelings about feeding

But it is probably your own feelings which most influence your decision about feeding, along with those of your partner and perhaps others in your family. When you discuss the pros and cons of breast and bottle as a couple, you may well be influenced by how much each of you wants to be involved in your babies' care. For you, the decision to breastfeed may depend on how you have felt when you have watched someone else breastfeeding, and on whether you believe it is possible for you to breastfeed two babies at once. If you want to get out and about with your babies when they're still small, you'll need to consider how you feel about breastfeeding in front of other people. It's less easy to be discreet with twins, so if you feel a little shy, you may find that you stay at home much more, where you can breastfeed with greater privacy. Bottlefeeding may seem easier in some ways but has its draw-backs, so you may have to take into account how much help you need and can rely on, or whether you are both prepared and able to share the feeding.

You may both be influenced by how you yourselves were fed in babyhood. Mothers and mothers-in-law often have strong views, and if you are hoping to enlist their help, you may want to take those views into account.

Advice from other parents of twins

Each method has its advantages and its disadvantages. With twins, you may find it harder to work out an ideal solution; you are the ones to decide which issues tip the balance, one way or the other. However, you may find it helpful to talk to other parents of twins. Their accounts of their experiences may make your own decision easier to take, even if on reflection you wish to feed differently. You can contact other parents of twins through your nearest Twins Club, your local baby clinic, your health visitor or your midwife. Your doctor's receptionist might be able to put you in touch with someone locally too. See if you can watch the other parents feeding their twins, as well as talking it over with them. Don't be shy, having twins is a great icebreaker.

Feeding premature babies

You may not plan to breastfeed on a long term basis, but feel that if your twins are premature or have to go into special care, then you will breastfeed for a short time to give them a good start. In this case, you will want to express your milk so that it can be given by tube or by bottle until your babies are able to move on to formula milk. You may appreciate the value for them of breast milk in the early days, but not feel that you want to go on breastfeeding once your babies come home.

Breast milk is the best sort of nourishment for small babies. They can digest it easily, and it gives them protection from infection. Babies' immune systems – that is, their ability to protect themselves from infection – are acquired in the last few weeks of pregnancy, so even strong, healthy, premature babies may be vulnerable to infection. Your breast milk, unlike formula milk, contains the antibodies which give them protection, feed by feed; so giving them your own milk can mean that you spend less time caring for sick babies and being worried about their health. Artificial baby milk is only an approximation of breast milk, since it originates either as cow's milk or as a derivative of soya beans. So if you decide not to provide your own milk the special care baby unit staff may feed your babies other women's breast milk from the hospital milk bank.

IT'S YOUR CHOICE: DOING WHAT'S RIGHT FOR YOU

Whatever you plan, your early choices are sometimes changed in the light of experience. In the end, whatever methods you may try, the essential thing is that you feed in ways that help you to cope best with the hard work of looking after two small babies. It can feel as though feeding is taking over your life, so if you are going to be taken over for a while, then let it happen in the way that satisfies you most and leaves you feeling good and confident that your babies are getting the best care and nourishment that you can give.

Although there are nutritional arguments in favour of breastfeeding twins, you may feel there are also practical and emotional issues which make bottlefeeding the best solution for you. If you are unhappy breastfeeding, your unhappiness almost certainly transmits itself to your babies and this destroys what would otherwise be an important effect of breastfeeding – that of bringing you and your babies close.

You can be flexible

Try to be flexible in your approach and see which method suits you best. You may try breastfeeding, while being prepared to move on to bottles if it does not suit you, and may then find that you continue for longer than you expected because you get into the rhythm of it and discover that it has other benefits. Consider starting with breastfeeding, because you can change from breast to bottle, but once you've started bottlefeeding you can't usually go back to the breast. If you've already brought up one child, you may already have a clearer idea of what suits you, and feel more confident about your choice.

BREASTFEEDING

None of the national surveys of infant feeding have looked at feeding twins, so there are no figures available on how many women breastfeed twins. Some certainly do, and they find it is possible to breastfeed twins completely for up to a year or more, never using bottles at all. Breast-feeding works on a supply and demand basis; the more milk the babies take, the more milk you produce. This means that once breastfeeding is established it can go on for as long as you wish. You may find you have plenty of milk for two babies without having to make any special effort. On the other hand, you may have to work quite hard at building up and maintaining your supply. To succeed you need to keep a careful eye on your own diet, eating and drinking well, so that your body has the resources from which to provide the babies' milk.

If you haven't enough milk – or are worried that the babies are not getting enough – and you feel that you can't boost your supply any further, you don't have to give up breastfeeding entirely. You can try mixed feeding (see p. 57).

Preparation for breastfeeding

When you plan to breastfeed you need to take extra care of your breasts during pregnancy and seek help for any difficulties such as inverted nipples.

For ease of feeding, make sure you have at least three good nursing bras, and a good supply of effective breast pads. Nighties which button down the front make night feeding easier and it helps to wear front-fastening clothes during the day while feeding is very frequent.

For the occasional bottle or drink of juice, you need four small bottles, teats and sterilizing equipment (see page 60). A hand breastpump is also useful for those occasions when you ask someone else to feed the babies. There are a number of different hand pumps on the market but those which work like a syringe are probably the most effective.

Many mothers find it enjoyable to breastfeed their twins simultaneously. It is important to support both yourself and your babies with plenty of pillows to help you all relax; it also helps when you have to wind one baby without disturbing the other.

If you decide to try feeding your babies together make sure you have lots of spare pillows to support you and your babies. It is a good idea to set aside four special ones for use only when feeding. If you put on plastic or polythene covers, underneath the ordinary pillow slips, the covers can be washed easily if the babies are sick, without soiling the pillows themselves.

Positions for breastfeeding

There are various different ways of holding your babies while you breastfeed, and your methods will change as they get older and heavier. Positions that suit tiny newborn babies become unwieldy with bigger babies; you may find you prefer to feed your babies one at a time after a while, even if you start off by feeding them together.

Mothers of single babies are advised to change breasts in the middle of feeds and to start each feed on a different breast. You can do this if you breastfeed twins, but because breastfeeding works on a supply and demand basis, it may be a good idea to keep each baby to her 'own' breast. If your babies have different appetites, this enables each one to set up the supply that meets her individual needs.

When both twins are hungry at the same time, you can try feeding them together. You may have to work quite hard to manage this, especially when they are very tiny. Simultaneous feeding might not be easy if they are still getting used to the breast and especially if they are still learning to latch onto and stay on the nipple. You need to make sure that their noses are not pressed against your breast and that they can breathe. You'll also need to replace the nipple in the baby's mouth if she loses it. You may have to put down one baby in order to wind the other, or to help one who is sick and needs mopping up. Both you and they get used to this in time, but at first it requires a lot of concentration, leaving you with little chance to talk to your babies or be sociable.

The illustrations on page 55 give some ideas about how to feed two small babies at the same time. As you can see, all the methods ensure that the babies' heads are well-supported and that you are able to cradle them both comfortably. You may find it easiest to feed on your bed; you could also try feeding in an armchair, sitting on a sofa or on the floor, supported by cushions and pillows. Experiment with these positions to find which one suits you best. Try to make sure your back and arms are well supported.

When he's at home, your partner can help you by making sure you are comfortable, and being on hand to wind and change the babies, especially if one feeds more quickly than the other.

Feeling close to your babies

Many mothers enjoy breastfeeding because they like holding their babies close and cuddling them while they feed. This can be a precious time for you, amongst all the chores and responsibilities that the babies bring. If you have been separated from your babies to start with, you may particularly value this chance to get to know them and to enjoy their closeness. Holding, touching and talking to your babies are good ways to feel close. But bear in mind, too, that however much you enjoy cuddling your babies, you are unlikely to feel this way all the time; feeding twins can take a lot of time, so you may feel tired or bored occasionally. You may like to use the time while you are feeding to read, watch television or listen to music. Many mothers find that this helps them to relax as well. You can even try some of the postnatal exercises that you can do sitting down.

BREASTFEEDING YOUR TWINS

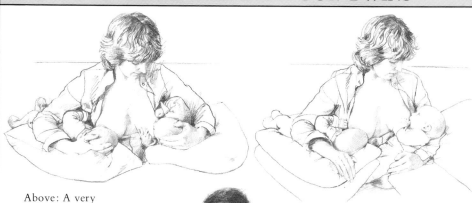

Above: A very comfortable way to breastfeed both babies at once is to lay each on a pile of cushions on either side of you. Their bodies are tucked round yours allowing you to cradle both their heads in your hands.

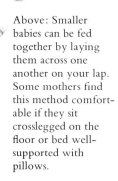

Above: A second method of simultaneous feeding is to tuck one baby under your arm and lay the second baby across your lap in the usual way.

Above: Smaller babies can be fed together by laying them across one another on your lap. Some mothers find this method comfortable if they sit crosslegged on the floor or bed well-supported with pillows.

Above: You may prefer to breastfeed your babies separately. You can feed one while talking and playing with the other baby beside you on the bed or sofa.

Above: Once your babies are feeding well you may like to lie down to feed, especially at night, using pillows and your own body to support their weight.

Feeding one by one

After the first few weeks, many mothers decide to breastfeed one baby at a time. You can put the baby who isn't being fed into a little chair, or have her beside you as you feed, and play with her while you feed the other. Sometimes mothers find that they pay more attention to the baby they are not feeding, especially if she is hungry and impatient to be fed. On the other hand, you may decide to ignore her crying because you want to give your attention to the baby you are feeding. If you always feed your babies in the same order, the same one is always hungry and ready to be fed before the other, and the one you feed second becomes less likely to cry and more willing to play or watch you while she awaits her turn.

If you have older children at home they may need your attention. You have not only to attend to your children and keep them amused, but also to cope with any feelings of jealousy they may have about your feeding the twins. However, when your partner is at home he can take care of your other children. Older children may enjoy spending time with their father while you are busy feeding. Fathers may also be pleased to have an opportunity to be involved by looking after one twin while you feed the other.

When there is no one to help you with feeding, and you are under pressure, you may try to find short cuts. For instance you could encourage the two babies to feed at the same time, or reduce the amount of time you spend playing with them. It's better to do this than to become anxious or guilty because what you expect of yourself is sometimes more than you can manage, and it may enable you to continue to breastfeed or to play more readily with your twins on another occasion when you have more time.

DIFFICULTIES WITH BREASTFEEDING

If you are breastfeeding, you may run into some problems. Even if your milk supply is good, your babies may not feed well to start with. Your babies, especially if they are tiny, may have difficulty in feeding. Tiny babies often do not suck well and are slow, erratic feeders. They are windy, inclined to be sick, and not easy to bring into a routine. They may need frequent feeding in order to get enough nourishment. This little-and-often feeding means that you can be feeding almost continuously in the early weeks, so you cannot help but be tired, especially if you had a stressful pregnancy and birth. You may also be anxious about your babies' well-being, and how you are coping as a mother. Even mothers with only one baby have worries and doubts when they are breastfeeding, and having two babies can increase them further. Worries like these are wholly understandable, but they can affect your milk supply.

There are other common problems with breastfeeding which can happen with any babies, twins or single borns. These include sore nipples, engorgement and insufficient lactation. There are a number of books which give good advice about dealing with these difficulties. If you want to talk to someone, you could try your local clinic, another mother of twins, or a counsellor from one of the breastfeeding organizations.

Insufficient lactation

Insufficient lactation is best dealt with by taking good care of yourself. Get as much rest as you can under the circumstances, and take care with your own diet; you'll cope with your fatigue better if you're looking after yourself and eating well. It's like a vicious circle; producing so much milk takes its toll on your body, and the more tired you are the less likely you are to feel like cooking and taking care of yourself. Your partner can encourage your breastfeeding by seeing that you eat well, by cooking or bringing in take-away foods.

The influence of other people

How well you establish your breastfeeding, and how long you go on for, depends partly on the other people around you. Friends and family may feel concerned about how tired you look, or about your weight, and perhaps worry that feeding two babies is making heavy demands on you. So even if you yourself feel good about your breastfeeding you may find their concern discouraging.

Of course feeding two babies is demanding. Perhaps you can re-assure them by pointing out that since you've got to spend most of your time feeding, it's nice to be able to do it in a way that gives you enjoyment and is so good for your babies.

COMPLEMENTARY FEEDING
The occasional bottle

If you feel, reluctantly, that breastfeeding all the time is too much for you, you may want to consider mixing breast and bottlefeeding.

One way is to give the occasional bottle. For this to be a successful option, you probably have to do it right from the start; babies who are used to the breast often object to bottles and teats if they are not introduced gradually. You can express your own milk and give that by bottle. This has the advantage of not diminishing your milk supply, while enabling other people to help with feeding.

If expressing your milk is difficult or distasteful for you, then mix up some formula milk (see page 60). Giving the occasional bottle probably has very little influence on the amount of milk your breasts are producing when you are feeding twins.

Complementary feeding is particularly useful if you are very tired since you can hand over the feeding to someone else. It can be especially useful if someone can help you with night feeds in the first three months or so, allowing you to get some unbroken sleep. If you cannot get help at night, try to find someone who can come in during the day so that you can sleep then instead.

Alternating breast and bottle

This is a good compromise method of feeding if you want to speed things up. The idea is to breastfeed one baby at one feed and give a bottle of formula milk to the other; then swop them round at the next feed. This way they both get a share of the breast and it is less wearing for you so you can go on breastfeeding longer. Your babies still get the nutritional and protective benefit of breast milk but it takes less time to

feed them and your partner and others can be involved. Later, it might make for an easier and speedier transition to complete bottlefeeding.

BOTTLEFEEDING TWINS

Many women choose to bottlefeed their twins from birth; others are unable to breastfeed, and still others change from breast to bottle. There are various factors that can make choosing to bottlefeed the right decision for you.

Some mothers of twins prefer to bottlefeed because they find the idea of breastfeeding two babies unappealing; you may feel embarrassed about breastfeeding two babies when other people are around, or feel that it makes you rather cow-like and that your body is not your own. You may find bottlefeeding less restricting; you can feed anywhere without embarrassment, and other people can help as well. Bottlefeeding appears less intimate than breastfeeding; there is less skin-to-skin contact between mother and baby, and less mutual touching and stroking. You may regret the loss of this extra contact with your babies, but you do have other opportunities to have that sort of closeness with them; for instance when you bath or change them. This less-intimate contact during feeding may be one reason why mothers who

Alternating breast and bottlefeeding for your babies at each feed is a good way of involving both parents in the care of your twins.

have children already are more likely to bottlefeed, since an older child may feel jealous and excluded because there is less time and attention for him, and twins decrease this time dramatically. This can be distressing, especially if you have enjoyed a very close relationship before the new babies arrived, or if you were in hospital for some time prior to the twins' birth.

Bottlefeeding and older children

Mothers sometimes try to help an older child adjust either by bottlefeeding or by partly breastfeeding and partly bottlefeeding. This reduces the appearance of intimacy between you and your twins, and increases the part the other child can play in feeding. If other people bottlefeed your twins sometimes, you and your older child can spend more time together and you can make a fuss of him.

Father's role

A special bonus of bottlefeeding is that it gives your babies' father a greater opportunity to be involved with feeding them, and encourages him to get close to his babies. Some fathers feel that there is not much they can do when their babies are being breastfed, but see more easily how they can help with bottlefeeding. If you shared each others' concerns and excitement in pregnancy and at the twins' birth, you may welcome being able to share the task of feeding your babies. This gives you some assistance and enables him to understand the pleasures and difficulties you are having to cope with each day.

Help from other people

Relatives, friends and neighbours can also enjoy feeding your babies. If they are inexperienced, they'll learn, and you can be there to watch what they are doing. Their help can free you for all sorts of other things that are important; not just more housework, but also for having a chance to relax, getting some time to yourself, going shopping or out for a walk.

Preparing for bottlefeeding

But inevitably, however many good friends you have, and however much the babies' father can help, most of the time it is probably just you who feeds your twins. You will also have to shop regularly for formula, prepare feeds and clean the bottles. The advantages of bottlefeeding become most apparent if you can make less work for yourself by organizing these chores efficiently or by sharing them between the other members of your family.

EQUIPMENT FOR BOTTLEFEEDING

Bottlefeeding twins requires quite a lot of equipment, and so is expensive. Even if you bought all the equipment for feeding a single child, you will probably find you need to buy more again for your twins. If you can afford to buy in bulk you can build up stocks of formula, bottles, teats and sterilizing equipment so that you do not have to shop constantly. It also means that you can clean a number of bottles at one time and prepare feeds for the whole day. You can store them in your refrigerator until they are needed.

Bottles do not necessarily have to be reheated before you use them. If you take the bottles out of the refrigerator about half an hour before the feed, you can simply give them to your babies at room temperature.

Bottles

Which you decide to use depends on what is available in your area, and on how much you want to spend. If you hope to cut down on your work by making up or sterilizing a quantity of bottles at once, you need a lot of bottles, covers and teats; probably at least twelve of each. You may think it is worth starting with half-size 150ml (4 fl oz) bottles if your babies are taking only 75-100ml (2 or 3 fl oz) of milk at each feed. Disposable bottles which come, already sterilized, as rolls of plastic bags that you fit into a holder and throw away after a single use save work as you sterilize only the teats and the covers. You will also need a large measuring jug, some plastic spoons and some bottle brushes to clean ordinary bottles.

Sterilization

This can be done either by boiling, or immersion in a sterilizing solution (available in effervescent tablet or liquid form). The bottles, teats and covers are placed in a large, deep basin, which should be made of plastic, glass or ceramic, but not metal as the solution corrodes it. Alternatively you can buy commercial sterilizing units. You might need two or even three of these as it takes at least two hours for the sterilization process to work. If you use the boiling method you need a pan with a tight-fitting lid large enough to hold all your equipment. Catering suppliers are a good source of very large pans.

For complete sterilization by boiling you need to be sure that the equipment is covered by water, that the lid is on tightly and that the water boils vigorously for at least five minutes. If you leave the lid on, your equipment will remain sterile until it is used.

Milk

At first you give your babies formula milk. This consists of cow's milk or soya bean which has been modified to resemble human milk so that babies can digest it easily. Most parents continue using the brand of formula that was given to their babies in their hospital. If you are not sure which brand to use, or whether to switch from one to another, try talking to other women who have bottlefed their babies or ask at your baby clinic.

GIVING FEEDS BY BOTTLE

When there are two people on hand, or you feed them one at a time, bottlefeeding twins can be much like bottlefeeding a single baby. However, when you are on your own, you have to find ways of bottle-feeding both your babies which suit you and them. Coping with two babies and two bottles can feel as though you need four arms and hands. Mothers use a number of positions for feeding; some find that they use one position most of the time; others vary their positions much more depending on how hungry the babies are, how much time is available for feeding, and whether they have to look after older children as well. When the babies are young you may be able to hold both of them to feed them. You can enjoy the contact, but with your hands full it's not easy to cope if one needs winding or is sick. When they are older you can feed them both at once by putting them into chairs and holding their bottles. This way you can angle the bottles so that they do not take

BOTTLEFEEDING YOUR TWINS

Right: Small but contented babies can be fed simultaneously side by side on your lap. You can support both their heads with one arm while guiding the bottles with the other hand.

Below: Resting the twins' heads against your body, and supporting their bodies on your lap or with cushions, gives you both hands free to guide their bottles.

Above: Another method of simultaneous bottlefeeding is to hold one baby and lay the other baby beside you with the bottle carefully propped on a cushion. Close proximity and a spare hand avoid the possibility of choking.

Right: Many fathers enjoy being able to help with their twins. Bottlefeeding allows both parents to feed; you could let a friend or relative help when they visit you. Two people speed up feeding and the babies each get some individual attention.

in too much air with their feeds, and you can easily pick up one for winding. It's a fairly quick way of feeding two babies. Neither baby is cuddled during feeding, but by feeding together you may create more time for cuddles or play afterwards.

As with breastfeeding, once twins are into a routine one may normally want to be fed before the other. This makes feeding and winding easier and you can hold and cuddle each baby as you feed her. But it takes a long time to feed separately in this way, so the waiting baby or your other children may become fretful. If so, you may want to try keeping her amused by propping her up beside you or sitting her near you in a little chair, or she may be pacified for a while with a dummy. When the first twin is fed and winded, then you change them over and start again. Once they are established in a routine, you may regularly feed one before the other, or you may prefer to alternate them.

Beware of propping up your twins with their own bottles before they are old enough and strong enough to hold them. Neither baby gets much attention; bottles may fall out of their mouths and small babies may begin to choke. It is a tempting solution for very tired parents but you must always keep a careful eye on both babies.

PACIFIERS (DUMMIES)

Babies derive a great deal of pleasure from sucking, and many enjoy having a dummy. You may find it helpful to use one, although it is not good for babies' teeth to dip their dummies in anything sweet. Some children become firmly attached to their dummies, but others give them up quickly or move onto sucking their fingers or thumbs. You may not have wished to use dummies with just one baby, but find that they are useful when you have twins.

WINDING

Some babies are more windy and colicky than others. If they do need winding you could try putting one on her stomach across your lap and one over your shoulder whilst you gently pat or rub each baby's back. Wind can be a persistent difficulty with some babies, and in this case you could try giving a little gripe water. If your babies have regular periods each day when they scream and seem to be in real and prolonged discomfort, they may have what is known as three-month-colic. For most babies this disappears spontaneously at about three months. If both your twins suffer from this trying condition it can be very hard for all the family. You could ask for advice about how best to cope with it at your baby clinic, but generally speaking it is something which babies just seem to outgrow.

WORKING OUT A ROUTINE

Some mothers are more interested than others in getting into a routine for feeding. You may think that you can fit everything in best if you know when to feed your babies, or you may prefer to let your babies decide when they want to sleep and to feed. The routine you try to set up is also influenced by other things; you may have older children who have to be taken to school at regular times; you may wish to ensure that your babies are awake and wanting to be fed when their father is at home; friends and relatives who are helping you may have strong views one way or the other. If you wish to return to work you may need to get your twins into a routine that their other caretaker can follow.

Some babies are easier than others to get into a feeding routine, and individually your twins may opt for very different schedules, so you need to be fairly flexible. Particularly when they are young, their feeding routines are closely tied to their sleeping routines, so see p. 73 for ways of getting them into a similar routine.

GOING ON TO SOLIDS

The introduction of solid food is often an important milestone for parents. Mothers are generally advised to give their babies milk until they are three months old and between three and four months most babies move onto solids as well, with bottlefeeding mothers starting earlier than those who breastfeed. Some mothers of twins like to bring forward the date when they first offer solids for the sake of convenience. However, twins, being small, may need to continue with milk alone longer than single babies.

When you start mixed feeding it is a good idea to give one twin a milk-feed while you offer tiny spoonfuls of solids to the twin who is still waiting to be fed. You can then alternate the process at the next feed.

Good foods to start your babies on are vegetables or fruits that have been cooked and either liquidized or sieved. Cereal is also a popular first food for weaning, and you could start with a proprietary baby brand, moistened to the consistency of thin cream with a little formula milk. Sometimes you may prefer to use commercial tinned or dried baby foods because they are convenient and quick to prepare – also important considerations with twins. If you are already cooking for the rest of the family you may like to set aside a little extra for the babies,

which you can liquidize or sieve.

Individual twins don't always like the same tastes and textures, so you may need to experiment and try out different foods to see which your babies like.

Giving solid food

Once your twins start eating solids regularly, you may find that you spend less time feeding them. You can feed them from the same bowl and with the same spoon, and they can sit side by side on baby chairs. Your babies may be thirsty when they have more solids and less milk, so you need to offer them water or well-diluted fruit juice as well as milk.

You may find yourself reluctant to let your babies take over their own feeding. Allowing twins to spoonfeed is sure to mean a mess. When your babies want to feed themselves they'll reach for the spoon and pick up their food with their fingers. You can lead them in gently by giving finger foods such as slices of peeled apple, toast, carrot or banana, but sooner or later you have to let them try with a spoon. The easiest approach – on your nerves and theirs – is not to care about mess. If you can find their antics funny, and enjoy their pleasure at manipulating food, you may find that the spirit of enjoyment makes it all worthwhile. If you really mind about the mess, try to put them where they can do least harm. Start by letting them spoonfeed at the feed after which they can most easily have a bath, and put newspaper under their chairs so you have less floor cleaning. You could try removing the trays of their high chairs and pushing them up against a table to cut down on the amount of mess. And remember, the sooner they learn to feed themselves the sooner you have less work to do!

WEIGHT GAIN AND GROWTH

Feeding can be an anxious time if you are concerned about whether your babies are putting on weight as they should. Indeed, some mothers bottlefeed because they feel more secure if they can measure carefully the amount of milk their babies are taking at each feed. It is possible to measure how much breast milk your babies are taking by weighing them before and after each feed, but this is, of course, more of a chore.

Parents of twins are intensely interested in their babies' growth and weight gain. When their twins weigh very little at birth, they are concerned to know whether they are growing quickly enough and whether they will ever catch up with babies who were heavier. These concerns can be increased by figures often quoted as 'normal' rates of weight gain, which refer to single born babies. A normal single baby gains weight fastest during the first three months, on average 200g (7oz) per week. This falls to approximately 150g (5oz) a week between three and six months. However, these figures are unlikely to give you much of a clue about what to expect with twins, and if you ask at your baby clinic you may find the answers given to you are rather vague or you are told different things. This is because there is little information readily available on normal growth rates for twins.

The growth rates regarded as normal for single babies are based on averages, but individual growth depends on the babies' starting point – that is, their own birthweight. The figures given above are the expected weight gains in the first six months for babies of average birthweight – – that is 3.5-4kg (7-8lb). Parents are also told to expect their babies to double their birthweights in the first six months, and to treble them by twelve months, but these expectations are not appropriate for babies of low birthweight. Premature babies who grew at that rate would be half-starved, and similarly, large babies weighing perhaps 5kg (10lb) at birth would be very overweight if they grew at that rate.

The majority of twins are of low birthweight. Their need to gain weight at a faster rate than average birthweight babies is yet another reason for their frequent feeds in the early weeks. They gradually make up their weight, but how long it takes depends on how small and premature they were to start with. The later their birth and the higher their birth weight, the quicker they catch up.

TRUSTING YOUR OWN JUDGEMENT

Whether it is feeding your twins or other aspects of their care you are thinking about, it is important to have faith in yourself. You may be overwhelmed by advice from other people and feel you should give it all a try. You may feel inadequate some of the time; most mothers do. But very soon you are the one who knows most about how to care for your babies. You rapidly become the expert when you have twins, because not many other people have them. Trust your expertise; it has been learned the best way – by experience.

It is help rather than advice that you are likely to need. How and where you get help depends partly on you; on whether you are the sort of person who can ask for help easily, or whether you are more self-contained and resourceful on your own.

At times it seems that the business of feeding is never ending. But it does get easier as the babies get bigger and are more able to feed well and as you begin to be more confident about feeding them. It is worth remembering that it does all come to an end. One day you will all sit round the family table at mealtimes and the days of breast or bottle-feeding will only be memories. Life gets easier and ultimately it does not matter how you fed them as babies when you have a close and loving relationship with two healthy children.

5 Caring For Twin Babies

While the amount of time spent feeding is probably the main difficulty for parents of twins in the early months, lack of sleep is usually a close second. Indeed the two problems are intimately related. It is the twins' need for frequent and often lengthy feeds, in addition to everything else, that can lead to your feeling so tired. The combination of incessant feeding and broken nights can lead to something approaching despair.

People who have not brought up twins probably underestimate the importance of having enough sleep at night in order to cope with their babies' needs during the day. As a mother of twins you have unprecedented demands made of you at a time when your physical resources may be seriously depleted by a tiring pregnancy, followed perhaps by a difficult birth. It won't be surprising if you feel exhausted.

In these circumstances you may feel inadequate and depressed, especially if this is your first experience of being a mother. The demands made on you are heavy – but nonetheless you do meet them. If you meet them in a way that feels less than ideal, it is not that you are inadequate, but that you are in a most difficult situation. There are lots of glamorous images promoted about mothering, including mothering twins, which set up expectations of how things ought to be. When your experiences do not match up with your expectations, you may feel cheated, without realizing that the fault does not lie with you. When you are very tired these feelings can all be intensified. What can you do to help yourself?

Being so tired

First and foremost you can recognize that mothering twins puts you under pressures that would challenge any woman. Your actual experiences may be far removed from your early expectations, and from those of your family and friends who know only about having one baby at a time. If you don't think that you are living up to your ideas of what mothers should be, don't blame yourself; instead, let those ideas go. Create a new image of yourself, of someone coping under difficult conditions. Allow yourself to feel pleased and triumphant as each day passes. Remember the new skills you've learned and new ways you have found to cope. Praise yourself for doing so well. If possible, talk to another mother of twins. You may discover that she and her babies' father are also finding it hard and are just as tired.

Secondly, you can try to keep in mind that this is a phase that passes. This is easier to believe if you have a child already. However, twins grow and develop at a slightly slower rate than single babies, especially if they are premature, so it may take them longer than usual to get into a sleeping routine. They may be awake more and they can be grizzly and difficult to quieten.

Problems of prematurity

How long it takes twins to get into a predictable sleeping routine depends partly on how premature they are. Small babies who gain weight slowly continue to need frequent feeds and take longer to sleep through the night than do bigger babies. Premature babies are more likely to be hyperactive, which means they may be compulsively active even when they are very tired, making it particularly hard to know what to do when they keep on crying. Sometimes parents are advised to give their babies a mild sedative to help them settle. Premature babies' nervous systems do not function so efficiently to start with, and their behaviour can appear chaotic and difficult to predict in the early weeks. This may be the reason why it is not easy to interpret their needs at first, and why they do not seem to respond well to your efforts to soothe and calm them. As they get older, things do get better.

Coping with fretful babies

Often there seems to be little you can do except sit it out as calmly as possible, and take a break, however briefly, whenever you can. However welcome and loved your twins are, there may be times when you feel you can't cope with the relentlessness of their demands. Some mothers say that they have to leave their babies in their cots and take a walk round the block to calm their nerves. Some mothers even get to the point where they feel they want to hit their babies; they are always miserable about such feelings, but they say that it has helped them to understand how babies come to be battered. Most people who experience an impulse to hit their babies never do; it remains only an impulse which passes and has no long term effects on their feelings towards their babies. Exhaustion does make people behave in quite uncharacteristic ways; if you do sometimes feel like this, try to talk about it to someone who understands and is not critical, who can help to relieve your feelings and reduce the tension.

**SOLVING
SLEEPING
PROBLEMS**

You may enjoy twins more if you are less exhausted and can increase the amount of sleep you and your babies are getting. If the babies are not being breastfed at night, parents of twins sometimes take it in turns to do the night feeds, allowing each other some unbroken nights, or they do the night feeds together so they do not take so long. If your babies' father finds it difficult to work properly after broken nights he may not be able to help on a regular basis but may be willing to take over when he is not working.

When it is not your turn to get up in the night, you may still be disturbed by the babies' cries or by your partner getting up to feed them. Some parents resolve this by sleeping in separate rooms for a while. Whoever is feeding the babies sleeps with them so that the other parent isn't disturbed. If space is limited you could try using your living room temporarily as a bedroom. Sometimes fathers feed the babies in the evening, or whenever they are at home, so that mothers can go to bed early or have a nap. However, if things are really getting on top of you, it may be possible for your partner to take a few days off work so you can get some rest.

All this can mean that you see less of each other in the first few months and that your relationship with one another takes a back seat while you concentrate on looking after the needs of your twins. Some parents regret this change, but others come to respect the new qualities they discover in their partners, and feel that ultimately it brings them closer.

Outside help

Understanding relatives may offer or be persuaded to have the babies for an occasional night, so you can both have a full night's sleep. If someone is prepared to do this for you, don't hesitate to accept. You can probably find ways to thank them later, when you are freer. Friends, relatives or neighbours can babysit for an hour or two or take the babies out. Try to use this time to sleep. If you aren't someone who can cat-nap or sleep easily during the day, at least lie down and try to relax, or do something that helps you unwind, like listening to the radio or to music. This is an occasion when your antenatal relaxation classes may come in useful. If you are normally a busy, active person, you may have to be quite severe with yourself. Don't always spend any spare time doing housework. Persuade yourself that a tidy house is no use if you are going to collapse in it. Put yourself as a first priority, for that is really what most helps everyone in your family.

If you have a toddler, resting may be difficult. You may have to go to quite some effort to get other children looked after. You will probably have to ask for help if you need it. People assume that you are coping and don't need help unless you ask for it loudly and clearly. Some women find it very difficult to ask for help and often there are very real barriers to making demands of people. You may think that asking for help indicates that you can't cope, that you are failing as a mother. It can take courage and you may fear refusal but once you've taken the plunge and asked, you may be pleasantly surprised by how much people are prepared to do. Many people are shy about offering help in case they are thought to be interfering, but are pleased to get involved if you make the first move.

The best place to look for help is within your own family, but if they can't respond try your friends and neighbours. If there is no one close who can help, or if they cannot offer what you need, consider contacting your local welfare services. Provisions vary widely from place to place but it is well worthwhile finding out what is available. There may be self-help groups locally which the Twins Club can put you in touch with. Having twins does not give you any statutory services as of right; you can ask for help, but you cannot rely on receiving it. Sometimes this is because welfare agencies do not understand that there is a need for help for some families with twins. It can also be that their resources are already overstretched, and they do not have any help to offer you.

Perhaps when your babies are older you could try to improve facilities if you feel strongly that families with baby twins should receive help.

PUTTING THE TWINS TO SLEEP TOGETHER

You could consider a number of ideas about how to get your babies to sleep more regularly and for longer. Twins are sometimes put into the same incubator after birth, with the idea that they have been together since conception and would miss one another if apart. You could try putting your twins together in the same crib or cot to help them settle and sleep. Some twins do seem to sleep better this way; maybe they derive security from each other's presence. Other twins simply kick and keep each other awake, so its a matter of trial and error to see what works best with your twins.

Twins can usually be left to sleep in the same room together. They rarely wake or disturb one another – it seems almost as if they are immune to one another's crying. However, if you think your twins might be disturbing one another, you may want to try putting them in separate rooms if that is possible. Swaddling (very tight wrapping) may create security as well, especially for twins who have been closely pressed against each other before birth. Different solutions may work at different times as your babies get older.

WAKEFUL BABIES

The amount of sleep people need varies enormously and the same is true of babies. You may be lucky and have babies who sleep a lot between feeds, and who wake obligingly at the same time. Identical twins seem more likely to do this than non–identicals. But the amount of sleep babies need also tends to diminish as they get older. Many first-time mothers are surprised when their babies have wakeful periods within the first two or three months of life and want to be amused and entertained. Toys or mobiles may attract babies' attention for short periods, but they cannot attend to things for long and they often become fretful and grizzly. This is a time when you may be glad of

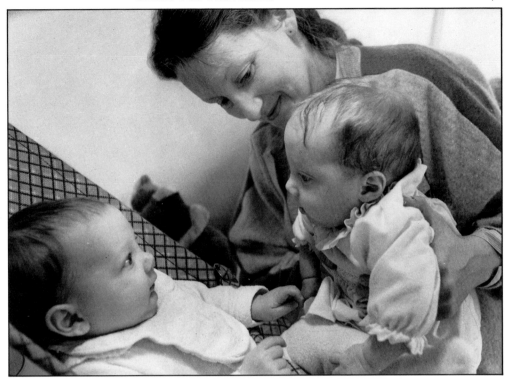

other people to help keep your babies occupied. It may help if you take them out; this sometimes amuses them, and may even send them off to sleep.

ESTABLISHING
A ROUTINE

Because sleeping and feeding are so closely related in the first few months, you may want to think about encouraging your babies to feed and sleep at regular times. The main advantage of having them in a routine is that they become predictable and you know where you are with them. This gives you a better chance of finding some time to get on with housework, see friends and pay attention to your other children. A routine can also help by giving you the feeling of being in control, rather than having your responsibilities dictating to you.

On the other hand, you may decide that you are not a routine-minded person, and that you prefer to respond to your babies according to their needs as they arise. This is becoming more popular as an approach to babycare; it emphasizes the individuality of your babies and accepts that babies differ in the amount of time they take to feed, how much sleep they want and what kind of daily rhythms suit them. You are encouraged to be very sensitive to your babies' behaviour and to be able to interpret what they want. It is quite a demanding way of bringing up children since it means that you accept your twins' demands and needs as and when they make them. If they are very unpredictable

Once babies are two or three months old, they may have quite prolonged periods of wakefulness when they need stimulation and play. Twins often find each other the most fascinating plaything of all!

and erratic it can mean that you are potentially on duty all the time. With twin babies, a total demand schedule can wear you out.

Even if you are normally very relaxed about having a routine or have already brought up one child without one, you may find your ideas changing when you have twins. If you can predict their needs it makes other aspects of life easier to organize; for instance, you can give your other children their meal before the twins wake hungry for a feed. It is also easier to arrange for someone else to look after them for a while if you have a good idea of when they are likely to sleep or need their next feed.

There are arguments for and against both approaches. If you don't have a routine but feed your babies on demand, you are incessantly feeding. If you are returning to work after maternity leave, it makes it easier for your nanny or other help to care for the babies if they already have a predictable pattern of daily routine. On the other hand, if you can cope with doing everything on demand, you have the satisfaction of knowing that you are giving your babies individual attention, getting to know them both and making the most of them. You are also doing what most babycare experts now suggest, which can be reassuring if you haven't had a baby before, and like to take advantage of current ideas about childcare.

You may like to have a routine in which your babies wake and sleep together because it makes it easier to get out. If you usually have one baby asleep and one who needs feeding, it can mean that you are always at home, watching over a sleeping baby and tending to a hungry one. On the other hand, if you feed the babies at the same time, you can be reasonably sure they'll both be awake. This gives you a chance to put them both in the pram, buggy or car, knowing that neither of them is likely to be hungry for a while.

It can take work to establish this kind of routine, and we suggest one way of doing it in the table below. Some babies readily conform to similar routines, but others are much more variable. You may feel that despite your efforts you'll never be able to predict when they'll sleep and wake. Even when you are successful you may find some days better than others. Being unwell, teething, nappy rash and other discomforts can all disrupt routines. Sometimes their formula doesn't seem to suit them, and you might like to experiment with other kinds of milk to see if it helps. But if establishing a routine becomes a burden in itself then the point is lost. It's then probably better to play it by ear, knowing that as they get older your children's daily rhythms are likely to become more predictable of their own accord.

EXAMPLES OF DAILY ROUTINES

Here are two examples of the way in which you can try to get your twins to feed and sleep at similar times, in spite of the fact that, initially, one twin wakes and wants feeding very much earlier than the other. The chart can be used as a guide.

TIME	FEEDING SEPARATELY		FEEDING TOGETHER
	Twin one	**Twin two**	**Twin one and two**
9.30am	Wakes and cries	Asleep	Wakes both babies if either not awake
10.00–10.30	Feed	Wake baby two, sit in chair. Talk to while feeding twin one	Feed babies
10.30–11.00	Sit in chair. Keep awake while feeding twin two	Feed	Hold, play with, talk to babies
11.00	Put to sleep	Put to sleep	Put to sleep
12.45pm	Wakes and cries	Asleep	Wake both babies if either not awake
1.00–1.30	Feed	Wake up, sit in chair. Talk to while feeding twin one	Feed babies
1.30–2.00	Sit in chair. Talk to and keep awake	Feed	Hold, play with, talk to babies
2.00	Put to sleep	Put to sleep	Put to sleep

Feeding separately   Twin one is kept waiting to feed, but hopefully the length of time is reduced. As she is kept awake and played with after her feed, she gets accustomed to the routine and starts to wake later. Twin two is woken up and played with before she is fed. She is encouraged to go to sleep after her feed, so she learns to wake up herself when it is time for feeding. Both babies are played with individually around each feed, and parents still have time for themselves between feeds.

Feeding together   Both twins are fed at the same time, one or both of them being woken up if necessary until they learn to wake up when it is time for feeding. They can be played with before or after their feed. If there are two of you, you can each play with one twin. In this way feeding takes less time, and gradually they learn to wake for feeding at similar times.

Either method can take weeks of patient work to get an easy flowing routine; some babies resist. If you keep a diary it might help you to feel that you are making some progress by noting small improvements as they happen.

Dropping the night feed   Another type of routine to work towards is the dropping of the night feed. If your babies are fed at approximately 6pm, 10pm, 2am and 6am, aim to delay the 10pm feed and to bring forward the 6am feed to start with. This needs to be done gradually, and probably shouldn't be started for some weeks with very small babies. Allow your babies to wait a few minutes for their 10pm feed one night and gradually stretch the time out until after a while you're feeding them nearer midnight. They will probably sleep through till 4-5am when you feed them again, and then not wake until 8-9am in the morning. In this way you encourage them to sleep for a longer stretch during the night, allowing you to rest as well. As they gradually take more milk at each feed they need more time between feeds to digest what they've eaten and the gap between the late night feed and the early morning one widens.

Routines and the family

Some parents try to encourage their babies to be awake and alert in the evening when their father as well as their mother and older brothers and sisters are around to play with them and enjoy their company. It also gives mothers or fathers a break if they have been alone with the twins all day. But if you both want to get out in the evenings, or to have time for yourselves or your older children, you may prefer the twins to sleep through the evening and be awake during the day.

RECOGNIZING YOUR BABIES' NEEDS

Whatever your views are about the pros and cons of getting twins into a routine, you have to consider how readily your own babies fit into one. In the first weeks of life any baby's behaviour is less predictable than it is later. Furthermore, all parents, even if they already have a child, have to get to know their babies, and to learn to interpret their needs. Babies signal their needs by different types of crying, different ways of moving and so on, and mothers are generally very good at recognizing these signals. Understanding what your babies want and being able to respond rapidly and successfully to their needs is a satisfying achievement for you, and it makes them feel secure as they learn to cope with all the new events and experiences of their early life. When you have twins, however, it is less easy to pay close attention to their individual attempts to indicate their needs. For instance, it may take longer for you to know which signs mean that one of your babies is hungry, or wants to be cuddled – particularly when they are so alike that it is not easy for you to tell them apart – and it may take longer still for you all to get to know one another.

Babies are individuals and some are more difficult to predict than others, so it takes more effort to get in tune with their rhythms of behaviour. Because twins are very often born early, with immature nervous systems, they can take longer to deal well with new sensations of hunger, noise, cold, warmth, light and so on. The signals they send out may be erratic and not easy to interpret. They may be very touchy about changes in things around them, like temperature or noise. They may sleep most of one day and want to be up and amused a lot the next. Some babies seem to find it difficult to make up their minds about things. Sometimes they love to be bathed; at others they behave as though they're frightened of water. Your twins may behave like this partly because of their immaturity – but they may just be those kind of babies! If it is immaturity, they'll grow out of it. If they're volatile personalities, they may settle down as they get older, or they may not.

Teething problems, coughs and colds or ear infections, can all interrupt even well-established routines. It is normal for this to happen, but when there are two who are feeling unwell and not sleeping it can drain your resources. Identical twins are more likely than non-identicals to be miserable with teething at the same time but at least you can hope that the disturbed nights may come to an end more quickly.

LEARNING TO SAY 'NO'

Because babies are born with the ability to signal or communicate their feelings it doesn't mean that you necessarily have to give them what they want all the time. If your twins demand endless amusement when you feel tired, you may decide to ignore them. Give them as much as you feel able to, and then say 'no'. It is not going to do them any harm if there are days when you don't comply with all their wishes, or if you sometimes leave them to cry. Even quite a long cry won't hurt them unless you're leaving them a great deal of the time. Fashions in babycare change, and if you ask your own mother how you were brought up, you may find that like most babies of that time you were kept to a fairly strict timetable, and fed by the clock, whether you cried or not. Turning a deaf ear to your babies' demands occasionally does no harm, and if it gives you a break so that you are more responsive to them later, it may even do some good.

KEEPING TWINS CLEAN

When you have two babies there are other aspects of their care which take more time. When they are also small babies, you have the extra concern about their fragility. It may take longer to build up your confidence so that you care for them efficiently and fairly speedily.

Nappy changing You do a very great deal of nappy changing with twins, so you want to make maximum use of the disposable nappies available. Nappy changing has certainly become much easier since the arrival of all-in-one disposable nappies with plastic pants, but if you have a good supply of terry nappies left over from an older child, it can make economic sense to stick with them. It may be cheaper to buy a set of terries than a year's supply of disposables, but you also have to consider the expense of nappy liners and plastic pants as well as washing, conditioning and drying. You may decide that whatever the relative costs, you do not want to add washing and drying to the task of changing two sets of nappies.

Disposable nappies, like baby clothes, are designed for the average baby. Your babies may fit into first size or 'newborn' disposables for some weeks or months. Some parents cut ordinary nappies in two using one half on each baby. If you do this, plastic pants with ties which can be adapted to fit the baby are probably best. Later, you can change to conventional elastic-sided pants for bigger babies.

NAPPY FOLDING

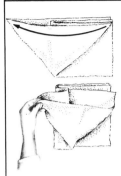

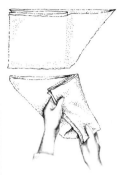

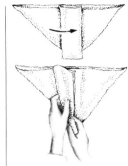

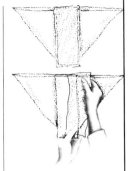

The 'origami' or triple fold nappy is the best method for very small babies as it gives maximum protection and is least bulky.
Take a nappy folded in four with free edges uppermost. Pull the top corner across to the left to form an inverted triangle on the lefthand side.

Turn the whole nappy over from right to left so that the point of the triangle is now pointing to the right.

Fold the two middle layers from the vertical edge at left over one another twice, forming a three-layer rectangle of nappy with triangular points on both sides.

Lay a nappy liner if required over the central panel and tuck it in on both sides to stop it slipping while you put the nappy on the baby.

To pin the 'origami' folded nappy, bring the two corners across to the front and pin through two layers of the central panel. This avoids any chance of pricking your baby's skin.
For extra neatness you can fold back the nappy at the top of the thighs before putting on elastic pants.

Terry squares come in a standard size, and are also too big for tiny babies who can look very undersized and pathetic with a great bundle of nappy round their lower halves. It is best to use the kite or origami method of folding for very tiny babies as it makes terry nappies less bulky. You can also buy shaped nappies which may fit better, though these are more expensive. If you use a sterilizing solution for nappy cleansing you need a large plastic dustbin because there are so many nappies.

Combining terries and disposables

You don't necessarily have to use just one or other type of nappy. The newborn size of disposables is a good choice to start with until your babies are big enough to fit into terries comfortably. There are times when disposables are especially useful; when you are out, when someone else looks after your babies, when you want to make a quick change at night, when your terries are in the wash, or when you do not feel like doing any washing.

Many parents of twins prefer to use labour-saving all-in-one disposable nappies. This means you have less washing and drying to do; they can also work out cheaper if bought in bulk.

If people offer to buy things for the babies, ask for a good supply of disposables which you can draw on. It is worth considering buying disposables in bulk; they are often available by mail order this way, which can be considerably cheaper and may save you some unnecessary shopping trips.

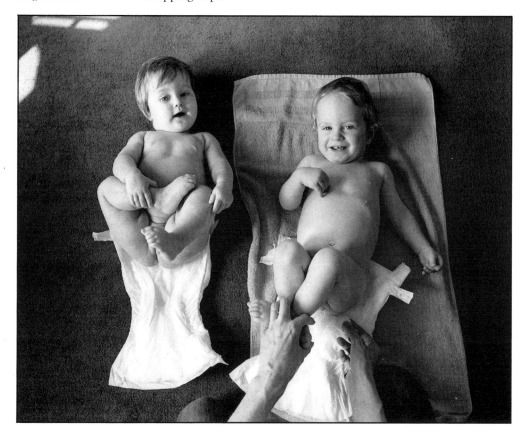

TOILET TRAINING

The advice these days is not to start toilet training until your babies are sitting up well and can be expected to have some control over their bladders and bowels. Your ideas about when your babies should be clean and dry may have developed round the care of a single baby, but you may find those ideas changing when you are faced with toilet training two at once. Only you can decide how important it is to get your twins into a routine and whether you prefer the effort of toilet training to that of changing and washing.

Persuading two babies to sit on pots can seem like a very hard task, so you may decide to delay it for some time, although some parents think it is worth trying to get their babies clean as soon as possible. Sometimes twins imitate one another, so once you've got one twin to sit on a pot or be clean, the other one follows her sister's example. Unfortunately, the converse is also true; the twin who is clean imitates the one who is not and you end up with two puddles on the floor rather than one!

You may try to encourage toilet training by giving your twins their own pots in different colours or by painting a special design or their names on them. Praise each twin when she uses it properly but try not to be cross when things go wrong – it can put them both off. One twin may be upset and frustrated if the other gets praised for doing something she really isn't ready to do yet. Children, and particularly children of different sexes, progress at their own speeds, so you may find your girl twin is clean before her brother.

Laundry

Whether you use disposable or terry nappies, you'll still have mountains of washing to do with twins, so make things as easy for yourself as possible. Make sure that everything you buy can be washed easily. Reduce to a minimum things like frilly dresses or pure wool cardigans which need handwashing or ironing. An automatic washing machine can seem like a life-saver, and although expensive to run, a tumble drier is very useful if drying at home is difficult.

BATHING

Bathing a small slippery baby is a tricky, time-consuming and often messy job. You may find that bathing two babies very frequently is more than you can manage on top of all the other work. Bathing one can be enjoyable, and the sight and smell of a newly bathed baby is lovely, but the fun may have gone out of it when you start on the second; it can just seem like piecework. Bath one baby when you're in the mood and leave the other till another day or until you have some help. If their father is at home he can bath one or other of the babies too. When they are small you cannot bath two babies together but later, when they can sit up properly, they can splash happily together in the same bath, or they can have a bath at the same time as one of their parents or their brothers and sisters. The kitchen sink can be a good place to bath small babies; you don't have to carry water about and you can stand comfortably. Meanwhile, you could settle for washing the babies' faces, hands and bottoms (topping and tailing) most of the time.

DRESSING TWINS

It is not easy to find clothes to fit tiny babies. Some mothers just put their babies into the smallest size baby clothes and wait for them to grow into them, but they can look a bit lost and comical in garments meant for average-size babies. If you search around you may be able to find a range of clothes made specially for very small babies. If you enjoy knitting and sewing you may be able to adapt patterns to your babies' size, or even use patterns for dolls' clothes. Once they get bigger finding clothes becomes easier. As long as they are warm or cool enough, it doesn't matter to your babies whether their clothes fit them or not. It may matter more to you, if you like them to look good. Twins are fascinating, and parents say how frequently they are stopped by people eager to admire their babies. At moments like that you'll probably want them to look special and a credit to you.

Dressing differently or alike

It is often tempting to dress twins alike, especially if they are identical. Quite a few parents feel its the natural thing to do; they like to emphasize their children's twinness, and think they look cute dressed alike. Even parents with a boy and a girl sometimes dress them in matching clothes. Consistent and easy recognition of ourselves by other people is something which most of us take for granted. Being recognized for oneself and called by one's own name are powerful ways by which our sense of identity is established, but this is often a difficult thing to do with twins, especially if they are very similar. Identical twins especially may find it difficult to sort out their own separate identities. If it is very hard for others to tell them apart – so that they are called by each other's names or simply referred to collectively as 'the twins' – they may become confused about exactly who they are.

Dressing your twins differently can help to ensure that they are treated as individuals; the more alike they are the more useful this is. Other people can recognize clothes easily, even at a distance or from behind. If your twins are regularly dressed in their own, different clothes, relatives, friends and, eventually, teachers, can get to know who wears what, which helps to take the guessing out of who is who.

Some parents plan to dress their twins alike at first, and then leave it to the children to decide for themselves when they get older. It does seem, however, that once children have got used to looking the same, they find it quite hard to stop. So, from the point of view of encouraging your twins to be individuals, it is better to keep dressing alike just for special occasions, and dress them differently the rest of the time. Even if other people give you presents of identical outfits, you can make them different by sewing on different motifs or embroider their names on them.

Teaching twins to dress themselves

As in so many aspects of their care, parents take very different stances about teaching their children to dress themselves. It takes a long time and a lot of patience to wait for a small child to get dressed; waiting for two can seem interminable. For this reason, parents are sometimes unwilling to encourage this kind of independence in their twins.

Once children start to dress themselves they have more of a say about what they are going to wear. If you've gone to a lot of trouble to build up two separate wardrobes and then find they wear each other's clothes, it may seem like effort wasted. On the other hand, the sooner they do learn to dress themselves, the sooner you are released from that task, so it's worth trying to be patient.

GETTING ABOUT

A complaint commonly voiced by mothers with twins is that they just cannot get out. For the first six to twelve months at least, you can expect to be very housebound as you feed and care for your twins. Only those mothers who return to work and employ full-time help avoid this completely. However, even temporary or part-time help does make a difference. If you have an *au pair*, mother's help or relative who can lend you a hand on a regular basis you will be able to get out to shop, or take an older child to playgroup or school. But even with help, your movements are probably going to be restricted.

Encouraging twins to dress themselves (or each other) is a time-consuming job requiring patience, but it is worth persevering since it will save you a lot of time in the long run.

If you have a twin pram, it is probable that you are restricted to trips around your immediate area and to local shops only. Using any kind of public transport can be almost impossible without help until the twins are old enough to walk and climb up and down steps. A car may increase your mobility but even with one you may find in the early months that the intervals between feeds are too short to enable you to get ready, go out and then get back again in time for the next feed. It takes a lot of preparation and effort, so you may decide to stay at home most of the time. However, with some organization you could perhaps visit friends and feed your babies while you are out.

Even with a small car, the many ingenious designs of folding twin prams and pushchairs enable you to get out and about more easily with your twins.

You may find you enjoy walking once you have twins because it is your main way of getting around. Twin prams are large and heavy, so try and avoid hills. Collapsible twin buggies are very useful, and a triple buggy can take a toddler as well. A good compromise is a double pram/pushchair with adjustable supports which allows both babies to lie or sit side by side facing you.

Visiting the doctor or clinic

One place you may find it especially difficult to get to while the babies are small is the doctor's surgery. You can ask the doctor to make a home visit; you may find your request is treated sympathetically if you explain how difficult it is to get out. Other places like shops or even the clinic may be difficult for parents of twins because there is rarely enough space for a twin pram or buggy. At some clinics you are expected to park your pram outside and sit with your baby on your lap while you wait to be seen. If you find you can't hold both babies for long, explain your problem to the clinic staff who may be prepared to bend the rules when they see your predicament.

Keeping in touch

You might begin to feel very trapped when you cannot get out as much as you wish. It is a major reason for the depression many mothers experience when they have small children. Getting your friends to come and visit you is one way to improve things; explain how difficult it is for you to visit them. If you don't tell them they may not realize. Keep in touch by telephone as much as possible, and ask your friends to ring you too.

Shopping

Many fathers take over the household shopping when they have twins. A frequent division of labour is for the babies' father to do the weekly shopping at the supermarket, while you take care of local daily needs. You may like to make use of convenience foods and stock up with things so you do not have to shop so often.

Toddlers

Older children can also be affected by your difficulties in getting out, especially if they are still toddlers. Your toddlers may find their social life severely curtailed by the arrival of twins. Try to get other people to take them out, otherwise they may get little fresh air or exercise and may make your life more difficult at home.

SAFETY AT HOME

As they learn to crawl and walk, babies point out all the potential hazards in your home. You may spend a good deal of time preventing them from hurting themselves or damaging furniture and precious things. Two children mean that you have to have eyes everywhere. You can respond to this by making your home more child-proof. Precious ornaments should be put away or placed on high shelves out of reach. Wiring should be checked for safety, and large mechanical appliances like washing machines should have childproof controls and locks. Keep poisonous household cleansers in locked cupboards out of harm's way.

It is also worth considering ways of restraining your twins; baby bouncers and walkers give them a lot of pleasure, and playpens and safety gates can keep them confined but still able to watch what you are doing. You may not have seen the need for such things with one baby, but even with well-behaved twins you may find them worthwhile. They limit the babies' mobility and prevent them from exploring but this may give you peace of mind and an opportunity to concentrate on things without having to watch them constantly.

RISING TO THE CHALLENGE

Twin toddlers mean extra care about safety in the home. Make sure electrical appliances have childproof locks and safe wiring, and keep bowls of pet food out of reach.

Twins do impose serious limitations on their whole family. However much you love them, they present you with a challenge at least some of the time. They make demands which force you to explore your resources and make the most of yourselves. You may find it reassuring to think that if you can cope with twins, you can cope with anything! Rising to the challenge may be difficult and exhausting, but may enable you to discover hidden strengths in yourselves. In this way, being alone with your babies, tied to the house for long periods and having little left of your former freedom can be turned to good account. You have every reason to be proud of such an achievement.

6 BRINGING UP TWINS

PHYSICAL
DEVELOPMENT

When twins are premature and small their growth and development may lag somewhat behind that of full-term babies. Slower growth is normal for twins; you can expect your babies to do many things later than other babies. We do not know how much more slowly they develop, since figures are not readily available about the normal growth of small babies or twins. If, for instance, your babies are five weeks premature, you can probably expect them to smile some weeks later than if they had been full-term. They may sit up, walk and talk anything up to three months late depending on how prematurely they were born. But they probably do these things in the same order as other babies. When your babies smile, walk and talk later than your friends' babies, it can seem like a big gap. You may worry that your babies will never catch up.

Catching up

It is not clear to what extent twins or small babies do catch up. In one study which looked at this question, it was found that children who had weighed 2.3kg (5lb) at birth tended to weigh 1.8kg (4lb) less at five years than babies who had weighed 4.1kg (9lb) at birth. Being nearly two kilos or four pounds smaller than another baby makes a difference at birth, but that difference seems very little by five years, and by ten years it's hardly noticeable at all. Similarly, being slow to walk and talk may seem important at eighteen months, but may be of no concern at all when your child is five years old. By then, other things become more important, like whether your child is quiet or chatty, calm or a fidget.

Very frequently twins do develop at different speeds at different times. Like these twin boys, you may find one of your twins walking several weeks before the other.

Other factors affect the rate at which children develop. One such factor is how tall their parents' families are. If you are all very tall, your

twins are likely to be a little shorter than the rest of the family, but still above average height. If you are all fairly short, then your twins are likely to be somewhat below average height.

Variation in growth rates

Your children's growth varies not just from that of single children, but from that of other twins, and even from one another. If your twins are identical, they probably grow at much the same rate. If they are non-identical, and especially if they are boy/girl twins, one may grow and develop more quickly than the other, and they grow at different rates at different times in their childhood. Early on, one may be up and walking, while the other one is still crawling. One may begin to talk before the other one. Girls often grow more rapidly in childhood, with boys catching up only in adolescence. So your boy twin may develop more slowly to begin with.

TREATING TWINS ALIKE AND DIFFERENTLY

In all families with more than one child the children have to share their parents' attention. The feelings of jealousy which parents some-times notice in a first child after the birth of a second are often caused by the need to share their parents' love and attention. When there are two or more children in the family it is inevitable that there is less attention for each one, but when one child is older than the other there are different things that parents can enjoy with each child. The individuality of each child is accentuated and acknowledged by the different activities you can share. The larger the age gap between the children, the more different are the things that you can do with them, so that in some res-pects the children have quite separate lives.

With twins, their age and hence their needs are necessarily the same, which means that you are more likely to treat them similarly, as a 'group' of two. When both are hungry you can sit them next to one another and feed them together with the same food. When both are crawling, the precautions you take, like gates and guards, are taken for the two of them. When your twins are of the same sex, and when they look alike or have similar temperaments, then it is even easier to treat them very much alike. If they both enjoy the same activities, similar toys may keep them both happy.

Your twins as individuals

Some parents try to treat their twins as individuals right from the start. They don't choose names that sound alike and try to distinguish their babies' differing needs and responses to things. For instance, you may find that sometimes one twin seems troubled by noise whereas the other sleeps through everything, or that one twin works herself into a state as soon as she is hungry, whereas the other is more able to wait.

But identical twins can be particularly difficult to distinguish, even when you have both of them in front of you. You may have to get to know them exceptionally well in order to recognize differences in their temperaments, or in the activities they prefer, which is why dressing them differently and trying to treat them as individuals is really very important. It is even hard to distinguish their voices sometimes, and you

It is particularly difficult for people outside their immediate family to treat identical twins as separate individuals. It is easier when the twins themselves show their different personalities.

may find it difficult to know which one is crying or calling to you if they are out of sight.

Boy and girl twins are much less likely to be treated in the same way, even less than same-sex non-identical twins. They still have similar needs because of their ages, but their different sex, appearance and perhaps more dissimilar temperaments may make it much easier for everyone to respond to their separate identities.

INDIVIDUALITY AND FAIR PLAY

Because their needs are so alike, twins do tend to be treated more similarly than other brothers and sisters. All parents are concerned to behave fairly towards their children, and not to favour one more than the other, but it's an issue which concerns parents of twins a great deal. You may have decided that you wish to treat your twins as separate individuals, but this may conflict with other ideas you have about treating them equally and fairly.

It is not always easy to make a distinction between being fair and treating the two children as though they were one. For instance, when it comes to buying clothes you may find it quite difficult to find equally appealing and similarly priced dresses or trousers but feel that it is unfair to spend much more on one twin than the other. In addition, something you do that seems the same from your point of view may not seem so to your twins. You may feel that you've been fair by buying the same toy for each child, but the toy might actually please one child more than the other.

You may try hard to play with each child for the same amount of time but if one child is doing something that interests you more than the other, you may join in the first child's play more enthusiastically. The children may be quite sensitive to this and realize that it's the genuineness of your interest that is important, rather than an equal sharing of time. You probably wouldn't expect yourself to be equally responsive about all the activities of a single child. You don't need to try to show an equal interest in everything your twins do, simply because they are twins.

SATISFYING DIFFERENT NEEDS

Even when they are very alike, children still have some different needs. One child may be a chatterbox and enjoy talking to you, whilst the other prefers to play quietly by herself. Being equally sensitive to both their needs may result in you talking much more to the chatterbox. Simply dividing your time evenly between them might seem fair in one way, but in another way it would be unfair, since you'd be talking less to one child than she wishes, and the other may feel her activities are being interrupted. However, what is fair changes from one situation and time to another. The child who wants to play by herself today may demand lots of company tomorrow. Being spontaneous and responsive to the actual behaviour of each child is probably fairer than attempting to keep a deliberate policy of sharing time and attention. It almost certainly evens itself out over the weeks and months.

Children are temperamentally different in various ways. Some children get very impatient and upset if they have to wait long for your attention. Others are more patient and equable by nature, and can wait for their turn more easily. You may find yourself dealing with the impatient child first because you and the other child prefer it that way. Parents often feel worried that appearing to have a favourite twin may cause the other one unhappiness. Being spontaneous towards your children and their differing needs at different times isn't the same as favouritism. They'll be in no doubt about how much you love them however you treat them at any given time.

PLAYING TOGETHER

If both twins are with you, an equitable division of your time and energies may be hard to manage. When you play with one child, the other may come and join in, interrupt, or interfere with the game. One twin may talk for the other, play with the other or work hard to compete for your attention. Many parents feel a bit defeated by the competition for their attention when they try to play individually with their twins, and are relieved if the children play together and amuse each

One of the great advantages for parents of toddler twins is that their similar levels of development enable them to play with each other, like these two-year-old non-identical girl twins.

other. Indeed, many parents encourage this and say that one of the good things about having twins is that they are company for one another.

Caring for pre-school twins is a time-consuming task, and there are other pressing demands on your time, so you may sometimes find yourself treating the children as a group, or encouraging them to amuse each other in order that you have a better chance to spend some time with your other child, your partner, or your friends. You probably feel that you need some time for yourself as well as caring for your children and running your home. Letting the children play together and amuse each other is one way of having a break, and treating them as a pair is another time-saver. For instance, feeding toddlers from one bowl and one spoon, filling each mouth in turn, is certainly treating them as a pair. But it makes feeding them much quicker. Few mothers would want to make more work for themselves by not doing this kind of thing. Finding a balance between doing everything together, and having some individual time for each child is probably what is essential, rather than attempting to do everything separately, or constantly leaving the children to their own devices.

BECOMING CLOSE FRIENDS

Their brothers and sisters are always interesting to young children. Many parents say how much easier they find a second child, who amuses himself by watching an older brother or sister. An older child may enjoy helping and playing with a younger one, but there is a limit to the amount of companionship and interest that children of different ages can offer each other. Bigger children don't always want little ones following along and slowing down their games, and younger ones find it hard to keep up. Twins, however, are always able to do roughly the same things. When one can stand and walk the other is also learning to be mobile. When one can play hide and seek the other can understand what the game is about too. This sameness can create very strong relationships between twins; it means that they always have plenty in common. These links can be further strengthened when people treat them as a pair. Being treated as if they have the same needs and temperaments can gradually make them more alike than they were to start with.

Being one of such a close-knit pair has advantages and disadvantages. Twins often become very close to each other, and are very central figures in each other's lives. The relationship between them can seem far stronger and more influential than any other. It is based on many feelings and experiences in common, and a profoundly intimate knowledge of each other. Their closeness gives twins an unusual opportunity to see how things look to someone else, an opportunity that single born children have only very rarely, perhaps through an exceptionally close friendship.

A twin always has the companionship of a child of the same age; they have a close and intuitive understanding of each other, and can enjoy the same games. Sometimes twins get immense fun out of things like sharing a joke that builds up out of their common experiences and understanding. Many of us, both adults and children, strive for and value highly such close and intimate relationships.

THE PRIVATE WORLD OF TWINS

The ties between twins can be much closer than those between other brothers and sisters, but this very closeness may set up barriers between twins and other people, even those near to them. Their mutual awareness may make them correspondingly less aware of others and less sensitive to them. This may mean that parents find their twins harder to control. Twins often encourage and stimulate each other to new heights of misbehaviour as their shared fun and their endorsement of each other's actions cuts out all concern about what other people may think or feel about what they are doing. This kind of behaviour may isolate them from the influence and companionship of others. Brothers and sisters may feel excluded and keep their distance. Parents can find that their influence is less strong because one twin seeks the approval of the other, rather than that of her parents.

These close ties can give twins great security, and are in many ways a source of strength. Many twins enjoy their 'twinness' and the pleasure it brings them. Having the constant support and approval of another person can be very reassuring as they grow and encounter new experiences. Parents often feel confident, for instance, about leaving older twins with other people, knowing that they have each other for security. They are less likely than single children to be worried by new situations or people, if they meet them together.

JEALOUSY AND COMPETITIVENESS

Being so close can also lead to jealousy and competition. As they grow bigger, some twins seem to develop a form of love/hate relationship. They may feel trapped by the very closeness that they enjoy so much. Struggles for individuality frequently take the form of fights and wild behaviour which then turns to mutual collaboration when an adult intervenes. It can be baffling for parents, who see their twins tormenting each other, but find they are rebuffed if they attempt to help. To be confronted by such closed ranks and to have to endure the power struggles and noisy wild activity of two children who are very hard to control can at times be quite distressing for the rest of the family.

Twins strive for individual and separate attention some of the time. Because they have similar skills, and can be very close, they may use similar, and often unwelcome, strategies for getting your attention. Fighting and having temper tantrums are ways of demanding attention. Parents' responses, and those of other people, may be to stop both twins at once. It's hard to cope with noisy or naughty behaviour from two children except by stopping both simultaneously. You can't easily attend to one child while the other continues to shout or throw things about. In this way the twins' efforts to get individual attention may be thwarted completely, since they've created a situation where they both receive the same, and in this case, usually disapproving, response. Sharing the discipline can help. You could ask your partner, or anyone else on hand, to restrain one while you attend to the other. You can then deal individually with both of them.

Some twins, even identicals like these, express their individuality strongly from quite an early age, and dislike being 'lumped together' as a group of two.

The Struggle For Individuality

Some twins struggle very hard indeed for their separateness and seem actively to reject one another. They may have abilities and aptitudes in common, but deliberately refuse to do the same things. If one plays football the other may show no interest in sport; if one plays the piano, the other has nothing to do with music; if one is sociable and outgoing, the other may refuse to have anything to do with people. Some of this may stem from the fears and fantasies that small children can rarely put into words. One young twin boy disclosed that he believed that because he was a twin he would grow to only half an adult. He thought that being half of a pair meant that he would remain half size.

With identical twins especially there are opportunities for such ideas to grow. Even quite small children can have such fears, and may show them by behaving in difficult and demanding ways. This kind of behaviour is very hard to live with, and requires a great deal of understanding and patience from parents and other members of the family. As they grow older the twins may find their feelings easier to talk about, and they may negotiate with words rather than fights. They probably need help to do this. If you can recognize that this behaviour stems from fear of twinship and being too close, you may feel better able to understand what is happening, and perhaps to cope. Making them look different and encouraging them to have separate relationships can reduce the struggle.

Learning To Talk

Babies are good at communicating with people long before they can talk. Crying, babbling, laughing, smiling, looking and pointing are all good ways they have of telling people things. Parents quickly become sensitive to what these messages mean; whether the baby is hungry, wants to play or have a cuddle. At some time, usually in the course of their second year, babies begin to add words to their messages. Family words such as Mummy, Daddy, cat, are often amongst the first to be heard. As the months pass, new words get added at a faster rate, and they are combined into simple sentences: Mummy gone work, there cat, want biscuit. These words and sentences are short and simple, but they are used to convey a wide range of ideas. A small child can use them to get you to do things; to tell you how she feels; to show you things; to ask questions and tell you about what interests her.

At first a small child's words and sentences may be difficult to understand, and you have to be in close touch with her world and what attracts her attention in order to make sense of what she is saying. This is something that parents, and especially mothers, are very good at, even without being aware of it. It's also very helpful for the child if people talk to her, echoing what she says and drawing her out. In this way children encourage adults to talk to them about things which interest them as children and this may be one way in which they learn the names for things. In turn, by having conversations, children can discover that what they have to say can be interesting to adults.

Talking to twins

Twins often fight for individual attention from their parents, frustrating your best endeavours to give them equal amounts of your time.

With single babies it's usually adults or older children who take notice of them when they learn to talk. For twins, things are different. Because there are two of them, adults and other children pay less attention to what each child is trying to communicate; instead twins themselves listen and talk most to one another.

It is more difficult for the people around twins to attend to two babies at once, to watch what each is doing, and so make sense of their noises, pointings and expressions. If you are busy changing one child, you have less opportunity to notice what is attracting the other child's attention, even if she is trying to show you. And if each child is trying to draw your attention to something at the same time you may feel you can't attend adequately to either, and perhaps you become less involved with either child's activities than you would if there were only one.

Parents often say sadly that they find themselves unable to pay as much attention to and talk to each of their twins as they would like.

With the constant presence of a second child, you may be unaware that one is trying, for instance, to show you the lights on the Christmas tree, because at that moment your attention is on her sister. You may ignore the first child's sounds and her pointing, or you may misinterpret them and talk to her about something else entirely. It may take her much longer to realize that what she finds interesting is of interest to you too, and the next time she may try less hard to tell you about it. Similarly, if one baby is waiting for her food you may talk to her and keep her amused, paying less attention to the baby you are feeding. In this case the baby being fed hears you talking to the other child about other things: your words do not reflect your actions. You would probably pay more attention to a single born baby while feeding, and would spend at least some of the time looking at him and talking to him. The experience would be more closely shared, and the baby would be more likely to learn that saying things and doing things often go together.

Having a twin to talk to

A single baby soon finds out that his parents are the people most likely to take notice of him. He can find out from them which of his sounds or sentences make sense. When they tell him by their responses that they don't understand, he learns to try different ways of saying things until he is understood. For a twin, the person most likely to take notice of her is the other twin. The noises a twin hears most may be the noises of the other twin, especially if there are no other children in the family. Twins may become their own best audiences. But of course they are not good talkers to start with, so they don't provide each other with good models of how language is used. They are unable to help each other learn which are the words to use. They cannot correct each other in the way a parent constantly does – 'No, it's not a dog, it's a cow.' Having a twin to talk to and share things with may mean that they listen less to people who are good talkers and take less notice of them. They are less likely therefore to correct what they say in response to what they hear other people saying to them.

The myth of secret languages

All children use the occasional nonsense word or use words wrongly. But usually, through hearing the words used correctly by older people, they come to use them correctly themselves. Very occasionally twins become such good audiences for each other, and understand each other so very well, that they become less interested in talking to other people at all. In rare cases this reaches such an extreme that they develop words or expressions that make sense only to them. However, even though they are well publicized, complete secret languages between twins are very rare indeed.

LEARNING TO HOLD CONVERSATIONS

You may enjoy watching your twins playing and talking together, and may laugh at the funny expressions they use with each other, but learning to talk is learning to communicate with other people, and not just with those close to you. All families have special words, such as names of pets, or expressions for bodily functions, which may not easily be understood by others outside the family. Learning to talk includes learning which words are special to some people, and which can be used more generally. It also means finding out the acceptable ways of saying things: 'Please may I have' rather than 'Give me'; topics which are polite: 'How are you? Are you looking forward to your birthday?'; as well as those which are unacceptable: 'Why is that lady so fat?'. What is considered acceptable or unacceptable is usually based on consideration for people's feelings and indicates respect for others. Most children learn these rules to a greater or lesser degree. Children who don't learn them very effectively often find it more difficult to get along with others, and may be less popular with both other children and adults.

These rules are first learned by children listening to what other people say and by trying them out. At first these are tried out on their families and friends and later, as they get more experienced, on people who are less known to them. Twins who form a very strong unit may be less inclined to look outside themselves for companionship and friendship, and so may experience fewer pressures than other children to learn rules and use them appropriately.

How to improve twins' language

Although twins' speech may start late and develop slowly, in time their ability to hold conversations improves. If you want to help that improvement it is probably useful if you talk to them separately. It's easy to forget to talk to your young children if you are very tired and feeling overworked; when it comes, peace and quiet may be precious. But it is mainly through taking part in play and talk with their parents and others that children learn language and how to use it. It's very helpful if their father, grandparents or someone else close to them can set some time aside to be alone with each child, to concentrate on talking directly to her, and to share her particular interests and activities. It need only be a few minutes a couple of times a day, but it is helpful right from the very beginning, when you first start taking care of your babies.

Giving twins individual attention

It's easier to play with one child alone if the other one is out. Try to arrange occasionally for one twin to go out for a walk and leave the other at home for some individual attention. When you are on your own you can put one child in a playpen or baby bouncer while you sit with the other to look at a book, do a puzzle together or draw. If you don't like to separate your twins, you can ensure that each gets an individual turn at whatever you are doing. Listen carefully to what each child says, respond to it attentively and look at anything she might show you or point at. Give her time to say more, or to ask further questions to which you try to reply before allowing yourself to listen to what the second twin has to say. With time they may learn to accept that each one has her uninterrupted turn.

Your twins' temperaments may affect how you behave towards them. If one twin is more talkative, or finds it difficult to wait her turn, you may find you usually pay more attention to her, which could explain why the other twin is less of a chatterer. Try to make sure you

give the quiet twin her turn, and that she is not always overruled by her noisier sister. Most parents do this naturally for one baby but with twins you may have to make more of a conscious effort especially when time is often so short.

When twins resist separation

The twins themselves may make it harder for you to put separateness into practice. If they are used to being good company for each other they may resist your attempts to respond to them one at a time. They may simply shout each other down, interrupt or play up so that one child's attention is constantly diverted from you onto the other. It's hard to be sensitive about one child's interests if the other is being naughty or noisy. If you can get them into the habit of having times on their own from an early age, they may be less likely to sabotage one another. Even if you don't succeed every time, it's worth trying to persevere. Teaching your twins these conversational rules can make quite a difference to their conversational competence later on. This in turn makes it easier for them to handle new social situations and new people.

When twins are separated you may find they can be miserable and uncertain, showing unexpected insecurity on their own.

SHARED GAMES

Twins always have a companion in play who is roughly equivalent in skills and interests. The extent to which they tend to be separate from other small children in their early years and the constant companionship they offer one another means that they can get into complex shared games. All children play at games in which they exchange roles, such as shopping and mother-and-fathers. One is the shopkeeper to start with, the other being the customer, and at some point they often change over. This may be a useful way to learn about the world and how to operate within it. Twins have an extra opportunity to share one another's worlds and to develop mutual understanding of each other.

Jealousy and competitiveness

Relationships which are so close can also give rise to negative feelings of jealousy and competitiveness. This is true of relationships between any brothers and sisters, but it can be even more noticeable with twins. Being so close to someone means that you know exactly what they can do that you would like to do, or what they have that you would like to have. You know how and when you can compete with them and win. Wanting the same toy, and having to share it leads to jealousy and fights, even when there are two toys available; the one possessed by the other child is the only one that is desirable. Unlike an older child who may be relied on to understand that a younger one finds it difficult to share or hard to wait for things, twins may both be equally impatient, and equally unable to make allowances for the other.

Interfering in each other's games

Having a twin to play with may add interest to the game, and help to develop complex, mutually understood rules and relationships, but a second child can also cut across the other child's games. In the context of play, children learn not only to co-operate but also to concentrate on things, to be self-motivated and self-contained. Playing by themselves enables children to explore things at their own pace and in their own way. Children need stimulation from outside, but it's also important to recognize their need for privacy and for opportunities to develop and learn at their own rate. Having a twin who breaks into what the other twin is doing, can break her concentration. It may also prevent her becoming confident in her ability to do things for herself.

Providing different playthings

Your twins may interfere with one another's play less if they are a boy and a girl, since they are more likely to be given different toys. Grandparents and friends may be more willing to provide different things for them, but may assume children of the same sex want to share the same toys. Whether your twins are different sexes or the same sex, providing two sets of toys may encourage them to develop their own interests and identities; for instance, you could provide lots of crayons and books for a quiet child, and bikes and balls for one who likes to rush around energetically. You may feel that this kind of individual provision is difficult, though, because bikes cost a lot more than crayons, and it may feel unfair to give more expensive toys to one than the other. To reduce the cost you could buy large items second-hand, and sell off some of your twins' toys when they outgrow them.

BECOMING
SOCIABLE

When you have twins you may think there is less need to take them out to mix with other children, as they have each other to play with. On the other hand, you may also find it easier to leave your twins together with other people or at a playgroup, as their companionship often makes each twin more confident about staying in strange places or with people they do not know. Occasionally, however, they may feel shy and self-conscious because of the extra fuss people make of them.

The more twins play exclusively with each other, the more difficult they may find it to make friends and join in the play of other children. We all have to learn to get to know other people, to be accepted by them, how to relate to groups, and how to make a gradual entrance into groups of new people, so that they make room for us as the newcomer. Belonging to a group or making friends is something we all work at, even though we are usually unaware of doing it. Twins, who are often used to the ebb and flow of their own 'group' of two, may have less incentive to watch others, to be sensitive and to take gentle steps forward into new situations. They may move over-confidently and roughly into a new group and either upset the balance of relationships between children, or appear to want to take the group over. Some twins do this with charm and are readily accepted; others are more clumsy and find themselves neither liked nor readily accepted by other children; some may tend to remain apart, outside the groups formed by other

The confidence they gain from each other's presence means that many twins are extremely sociable and outgoing. They take in their stride new experiences like birthday parties, which may be more of a challenge to a child on his own.

children. These issues sometimes arise when they first go to school and adjust to school life and to other children within the class. Teachers have a useful role here in helping those who don't settle in readily.

CONFIDENCE AND VULNERABILITY

Your twins have less experience of mixing on their own than do other children. A single child may be most anxious when he is left on his own without his mother; staying on his own at playgroup may be quite frightening at first, however much he later enjoys himself. Twins may be less afraid when their mother first leaves them with other people because they have each other. This can give everyone the impression that they are very confident children, but when one twin is left somewhere without the other, she may suddenly appear anxious and worried. This may come as a surprise if you are used to their confidence when they are together. Twins may mask each other's vulnerability, and this is something to bear in mind when making arrangements to have them looked after. Their apparent security may be quite illusory. They may be just as much in need of your support and presence in new situations as a single child. Their need may be well-disguised by their confidence at home as a pair. In fact, they may disguise their insecurity so well that they create an appearance of not needing anyone outside themselves, putting stronger barriers between themselves and you. Encouraging them to develop in different ways allows them to express their need for

your support and love and that of other adults.

The more your twins lead separate lives the more you give them opportunities to tell you that they do need you. Showing how vulnerable we are can be frightening; there's always the possibility of being rejected. If twins do not have a chance to come to accept their vulnerability as small children, they may be unable to do it as adults, and this can affect their ability to create relationships as they grow older. It may limit their capacity to be open and to trust others and to recognize and respond to trust and need.

Mixing with other children

Once they go to school, twins mix with other children, but you may like to give them the opportunity before then. This ensures that they have the chance as early as possible to learn how to get along with other children and adults and to cope with new situations on their own. Another reason for giving them separate experiences while they are young is that it encourages other people to get to know them as individuals. In this way the twins themselves may be helped to think of themselves as separate people.

SWITCHING ROLES

Sometimes twins take on 'roles' within their relationship. One becomes the dominant member or leader, and the other the submissive member, or follower; one sometimes becomes the talker and one the listener; one may be the good and well-behaved twin and the other the naughty one. Sometimes these roles become stable, so that the children behave consistently in these ways and they become part of their personalities, even when the other child is absent. More often, though, they seem to switch roles, sometimes very rapidly. Twins do this more frequently and more adeptly than other brothers and sisters. Knowing so much about each other's worlds and about each other's messages, they seem to know what the other twin is thinking.

Compared with other members of their family, twins often excel at 'Guess what I'm thinking' games because of their understanding of each other's messages, both verbal and non-verbal. It is this understanding which allows them to switch roles so quickly. One morning one twin is bossy, and the other allows herself to be lead, but by the afternoon they have changed roles, and the bossy one is now allowing herself to be told what to do. These roles may also be maintained over long periods. When they are eventually exchanged it comes as a surprise to the people around them, who have got used to thinking of them in the former way. Sometimes they seem so adept at role switches that you almost believe in extra-sensory perception. However, despite many stories of twins, especially identical twins, behaving in the same way and doing the same things even when they are miles apart, there is little evidence that twins do have ESP.

Identity confusion

When twins act in unison or swap roles, it makes it more difficult to maintain a clear impression of their separateness. Without this awareness other people can often confuse their personalities, especially when the twins are the same sex. It's easy, for instance, to call them by the wrong name, even when they do not look very alike. To avoid this, people quite often call them by a group name, such as 'the twins' or 'the Smiths'. Many twins find it upsetting to be confused with each other in this way, and it may discourage them from venturing out beyond the small world where everyone can distinguish them. It's not easy to explain to young twins how their own behaviour contributes to other people's misunderstandings, but you can ensure that they have some opportunity to develop separate friendships and relationships. Try to encourage and enhance some of the features which the twins themselves feel distinguish them. For instance, if one is a smart and snappy dresser, you might want to encourage her interest in clothes, and help her build friendships with children who respond to these aspects of her personality.

ILLNESS AND ACCIDENT

Twins may feel more isolated and anxious than other brothers and sisters when one of them is ill. One child's identity may be so heavily based on the presence of the other that illness and injury to one twin may seem like illness or injury to the other. Some twins do seem to be touchingly concerned for each other, ready to nurse and show a great deal of sympathy for the sick twin. On the other hand they may be quite indifferent. Like other young children, twins can be self-centred and unwilling to tend to the needs of others.

The impact of the illness of one of the twins on the other comes about, too, because it results in a disruption of the life the two share. Their day-to-day activities are very interdependent, and when one twin is ill the other loses her companion. Twins who are rarely alone may appreciate having their twin out of the way for a while. It also gives parents an opportunity to have time alone with each of them. Despite the anxieties illness may bring, it can sometimes be turned to good account. If one twin has to go into hospital then the two children are separated from one another. Most hospitals make provision for regular visiting by parents, but only a few welcome brothers and sisters so readily. A twin in hospital may need her twin as much as her parents, to speed her recovery and maintain her links with her family. Taking photographs, favourite toys, or passing messages, drawings, or notes from one twin to the other helps to keep them reassured about one another. It's clear that the twin in hospital is missing her family, but the loss experienced by the twin left at home and her need to keep in contact needs to be recognized as well.

The strength of their ties on the other hand may help to protect them against losses which single children may find harder to bear. One such loss is when their mother goes into hospital. Having a twin for support and company may result in a less painful time for your twins than for your single children. It's always impossible to generalize about such feelings of course. Some twins, like some single children, are better able to cope with illnesses and losses than are others.

DISCIPLINING TWINS

Parents often have quite strong views about how important they think it is for their children to be well-behaved. Whether you think of yourself as a strict or tolerant parent depends as well on what kind of behaviour you are considering. Temper tantrums, fighting, telling tales, answering back. being very noisy, breaking things, bad table manners and sexual exploration can all annoy parents. Parents differ considerably in the behaviour they consider intolerable, and in the ways they discipline their children. Your ideas about discipline change frequently in the light of experience and according to your children's temperament. You may give up the fight against bad table manners because your children resist all your attempts to teach them good ones. Or you may find that although you never intended to send your children to their rooms as a punishment, you do so because it works with them or because you underestimated how important a few moments of quiet are to you.

Issues to consider

With twins there are a number of issues which you need to consider. Certain aspects of their twinness give them the potential for unacceptable behaviour, whether their intention is to be naughty or not. A child who is inclined to temper tantrums may react by having more and more temper tantrums if there are consistent delays in meeting her needs. With a single child it may be easier to ward off the temper tantrums by dealing with the child's needs more promptly, but with two children this is more difficult. Because your attention is divided you may be less aware of the tell-tale signs of a coming tantrum or you may not be able to finish what you are doing with the other twin quickly enough to deal with her sister in time.

The jealousy between twins may be exaggerated when they are always aware of the other one being fed, cared for or played with. This jealousy may erupt into aggression and violence. Another response may be to try to get the other twin into trouble. Knowing each other so well can make it easier to think of hurtful remarks or weak points, so one twin may cajole or taunt the other until she gets angry, shouts or becomes violent. Parents may well assume that the twin who is shouting is the troublemaker and punish her more than the twin who started off the round of naughtiness. Equally the confidence your twins have as a pair may encourage them to behave in unacceptable ways, such as taking over other children's activities or bossing other children around. You may not like them to behave like this and you may also fear that it is likely to end in shouting, damage or aggression.

Thoughtless behaviour

Twins' behaviour may be less influenced and controlled by concern about what other people may think. One twin may help the other one into mischief and together they may collaborate to create more trouble than either twin could tolerate on her own. For instance, one mother tells of how her first twin started an uproar by repeatedly slamming a door shut. As one twin stopped, her brother took up the task, repeatedly slamming an adjacent door. Both children encouraged the other's behaviour so that the disapproval of their mother who came in part way through was lost upon them. At some point during naughty behaviour, most children stop in shock at the destruction they have caused or they begin to feel anxious about how others will react. The presence of the other twin supporting and encouraging the misbehaviour seems to prevent this happening so quickly.

When your children frequently go beyond the bounds of what's considered reasonable or tolerable behaviour, you may feel your standards and even your competence as a parent are being challenged. Temper tantrums at the supermarket check-out or fights in the bus queue are very conspicuous. When their children behave badly, especially in public, parents can feel very inadequate and twins are more noticeable than single children. One of the great rewards in having twins is the interest and delight they inspire in other people, but because twins are always noticed, so too is their bad behaviour and badly behaved twins are doubly threatening to their parents' feelings of self-worth.

The effect of punishment

Parents have two concerns about discipline; one is the effectiveness of the punishment and the other is the effect that punishing one twin has on the other. There may be a limited number of ways in which you can penetrate the unit of two. Bear in mind that your punishment of one may be ineffective if the second one continues to support the first one in her naughtiness. Showing you are cross, shouting at her or even sending her to bed early may not work if the second twin smiles and winks her approval. Occasionally brothers and sisters support one another like this but it seems to happen more frequently with twins. One of the most effective responses to this is to separate them before attempting to discipline them. This also avoids the problems that can arise from one twin observing the other being punished. The twin who is not punished but who watches the other may relish the sight. On the other hand she may find it very painful. Their close ties can make it feel almost as if she is the one being punished, as well as her twin.

PLAYGROUPS AND SCHOOLS

We have already suggested that it is important for twins not to become too engrossed in themselves but to develop separate identities. If there are brothers and sisters in the family they may help the twins to move beyond themselves to think and care for other children. But they also need experience with children with whom they are not so closely involved. Friends' or neighbours' children at a local playgroup can help them to learn the skills of making and keeping friends. The ideal would be for your twins to attend different playgroups, or the same one on different days; unfortunately there are rarely enough playgroups in the locality to make this possible, and if there are it requires a lot of organization. Instead explain to the playgroup leader that you would like the staff to encourage the twins to play separately as much as possible in order to encourage their individuality.

Playgroup activities are as important for twins as they are for all children. Your twins may stick together without mixing with the other children (right). You could ask the playgroup leaders to encourage them to join in with other children (below) and develop their individual skills.

Separating Twins At School

One way of helping your twins develop their own identities and friendships is by separating them when they go to school. If the local school has two classes in each year, or some other flexible arrangement, you may want to consider putting them into different classes. Many infant schools are too small for this, so you would have to send them to different schools to have them in different classes. As with playgroups, this may be difficult to arrange, and you may prefer to encourage their individuality in other ways through clubs and out-of-school activities.

If you want your twins to be separated at school, you need to explain why you prefer it to the teaching staff. It is often assumed that parents want their twins to be educated together. The staff may be puzzled at first because your request is unusual, but once they understand your reasons, they may be happy to co-operate. Also explain to the teachers how and why you try to treat your twins alike and differently. They may not have thought much about how to treat twins and may be pleased to follow your example. Teachers have large numbers of children to take care of and it can be difficult to deal with them all as individuals. If your twins are very alike you could help the staff by giving them name labels when they first go to school. If the twins are to be in the same class it is useful for the teacher to know of any distinct interests and skills. They are then less likely to be given the same work to do all the time, and may be encouraged to join different groups in the classroom, reinforcing the efforts you have already made to develop their separate identities.

7 Twins And The Family

Having twins is a specific and unique experience. It is not at all like having two children born close together; this is something that is hard to explain to people who have not had twins themselves. Many parents feel proud and pleased about having twins, and enjoy the interest and attention they attract. Inevitably though, they have mixed feelings as well, for there are big adjustments to be made both physically and emotionally. As one mother put it sadly, 'There are so many times when I would give anything to have both of them, but as one. I couldn't choose between them, but if I could make both of them into one, that's what I really want.' Like so many parents, she felt that she could not spend as much time with each of her twins as she wished, because there were two of them.

Being the centre of another person's world, and especially a person as dependent and vulnerable as a baby, is enormously rewarding. Feeling that you are needed can sustain you through sleepless nights, baby-filled days, and the changes that becoming parents bring. Twins, however, can become the focus of each other's life and interest, and they may develop in ways that make you feel excluded and less needed. If you begin to feel less central to their lives you may, regretfully, leave your twins more and more to their own devices, especially if you are tired and cannot find much time for yourselves.

Twins give both parents a unique opportunity to share in the upbringing of their children. A baby sling each is one way of going out together.

There may be times when you would like to talk about your negative as well as positive feelings. You may feel, however, that people do not understand and are not prepared to talk about them, but reply with

comments like 'Oh, I've always wished I'd had twins, it must be such fun'. It can of course be great fun and many families certainly get a great deal of joy and happiness from having twins.

FATHERS'
INVOLVEMENT

Fathers can have a very important role to play in bringing up twins. With two babies it is even more obvious how much work there is to do; fathers can see more clearly what they can do, and mothers especially appreciate their support. Your ideas about how much fathers should be involved in child care may change when there is so much work to be done. Fathers who have always wanted to be closely concerned in the care of their babies enjoy the opportunity they have to get to know their children, and to learn to look after them. Even when your babies' father is at work you may both want to consider ways of ensuring that he doesn't feel left out. He can still help with feeding, changing, bathing, playing, reading the twins bedtime stories and taking them out. If he takes out one twin or stays at home with one while you go out, both twins have a chance to be with one of their parents by themselves. Many fathers take on responsibility for shopping and sometimes for cooking and housework too; they look after their twins, take time off work if necessary for doctor's appointments, check ups, dentists visits, etc., and take over to give you time to catch up on sleep or have time to yourself.

However, if you are a single parent, or your babies' father does not take an active share in bringing up your twins, you may want to ask relatives, friends and neighbours to help you with the extra work the children bring.

ADJUSTING AS
A COUPLE

You also have adjustments to make as a couple. The arrival of a baby in the family always brings changes in parents' lives; when you have twins the changes are greater. The impact on your lives is somewhat different depending on whether or not you have children already. When twins are the first-born in a family, you have more time to rest and do not have to consider the needs of older children as well as yourselves and the babies. When you already have children, you may feel more able to take twins in your stride, even though you have the others to care for. It probably depends on the age of your children; the wider the age gap, the more independent your older children may be and more able to enjoy having twins for brothers and sisters.

Whichever of you has the primary care of your children because of job arrangements, you may occasionally have mixed feelings about your partner's relationship with them. Small children have a way of seeming to take the parent who looks after them most of the time for granted. You may feel jealous when children who have been a handful all day are excited and pleased when your partner comes home and plays with them, and it can be upsetting to feel you have to compete with your twins for your partner's attention. You may feel this way even when you are pleased that your partner is involved and you enjoy

A father of twins can take an active part in childcare especially at bedtime if he has been out at work all day. He can undress them, supervise their bath and read a bedtime story. This can give their mother some welcome time to herself if she has been at home all day with them.

being able to relax while someone else takes over their care.

Once you have a baby your relationship with your partner inevitably changes. You have less time for one another and the extra work of looking after two babies means that you may be less able to share your thoughts and feelings. If you look after your babies most of the time, you may feel very housebound and envious of your partner being able to leave the children and the chores behind.

Many other factors contribute to changes in your relationship. Spending so much time at home, you may come to rely on those close to you, and especially your partner, for companionship and contact with the outside world. Few new parents have very clear ideas about how they will manage on a day-to-day basis; you may worry about the extra expense and responsibility twins bring. If you've always thought of one another as capable and independent, it might be quite a new experience to see each other having difficulty in coping. It may take time and effort to adjust to these new sides of each other's personalities and to help one another learn new ways of being supportive and caring.

Some men find these adjustments particularly difficult, in which case you may have to consider carefully what you most need your babies' father to do. It may take time to work out the ways in which both of you can best take care of your children and take care of each other. Even when the physical side of your relationship is at rather a low ebb, getting to know more about one another as parents can bring you closer together.

Sexual relations   You may find it takes time for your sexual relationship to adjust. Sexual intercourse may not seem very inviting, especially if you are still convalescing after your twins' birth. However, you and your partner may be longing to be close again, especially if you were in hospital for a long time before the birth, or had been advised to refrain from sex for some months. With patience and understanding you can be close to one another; physical contact can be reassuring and comforting for its own sake, and you may be able to satisfy each other's sexual needs even when intercourse is too uncomfortable. However, even when you have recovered physically from the birth, you may both be too tired to bother, so you may not see this as a problem but feel content to wait a while.

Contraception   It is still important to think about contraception (even though twins may seem like the best method ever invented!). Remember that it is not true that you can't conceive while you are breastfeeding. In this case you may be advised to use a low progesterone pill or to have an IUD inserted, since the ordinary contraceptive pill can slow up your milk supply. If you had your twins after treatment with ovulation-inducing drugs or after a number of miscarriages, you shouldn't assume that you won't get pregnant again. Having problems in conceiving before you had your twins is not necessarily an indication that you'll have problems another time. Do ask for contraceptive advice at your post-natal check up, or even earlier, whilst you are still in hospital after your delivery.

Enlarging your family   Having twins may alter parents' feelings about wanting more children. When twins are your first children, you may wish to have another child, even when you thought you would only want two children. You may regret not having the one-to-one relationship you have with one baby. But parents who have already enjoyed this kind of relationship with their children may decide to let their twins complete their family.

As a result of treatment, some twins are born to women who have adopted children after a long history of infertility. If your twins are born into a family of adopted children, you'll find ways of reassuring them as they grow up that you love and want all your children as much as one another.

OLDER BROTHERS AND SISTERS   An older child may feel doubly displaced by the arrival of twins. The needs of twins, especially if they are sickly or demanding, can drain the rest of your family and leave you with little time or energy for older children. If you were admitted to hospital antenatally and had to leave your children for some time, it may take quite a long time to get to know them again and to regain their trust and security. They may feel angry and upset that you left them and then came home with two babies.

Because twins can be born early it sometimes happens that you come home, leaving them in hospital. This can be puzzling for a toddler or older child, who knows that you were in hospital because there were to be new babies, but who sees you come home without them. It may be hard for a small child to understand what has happened. Indeed this may be a difficult time for the whole family. If your children have visited the hospital and seen the babies, they may have odd ideas about why they have been left behind. They may not understand that the babies will come home, so that when they do it's a shock. If very premature, twins can stay in hospital for many weeks after their birth. During that time life for your toddler can seem to return to normal, making it even more of an adjustment when the babies do arrive home. Your older child may feel angry and upset, although he may find his feelings difficult or frightening to express. He can be especially in need of love and understanding, as in a sense he has a double adjustment to make; of you going away to have the babies, coming home without them and then of their arrival later. He probably also has to accept that they take away a great deal of the attention that has been his in the meantime.

Some of the time older brothers and sisters become more grown-up when the twins arrive home. At other times they might feel like being babies again, so that, for instance, a child who was dry has to have nappies once more. This may happen because your children are upset and don't understand why their parents, and especially their mother, have less time for them when there are new babies to care for. They may miss having to themselves as much as they used to do. This may be an easier adjustment for children old enough to have friends of their own, but may be more difficult for older children who are still only toddlers themselves.

Older brothers and sisters often feel more grown-up when twin babies arrive. This girl and boy each 'adopted' one of their twin brothers and gave them special attention.

Feeding and siblings

Second-time mothers are less likely to breastfeed than are first-time mothers. Although the reasons for this are not entirely clear, they may be partly connected with the conflict between the demands of the older child and the new baby, or in the case of twins, two babies. It is another factor which parents of twins have to weigh up when deciding whether to breastfeed or bottlefeed (see page 50).

When you have an older child you may feel that breastfeeding makes unacceptably heavy demands on you. There are some short cuts, like simultaneous or complementary feeding, which reduce the amount of time you spend with the twins. If you really want to breastfeed, these compromises may seem sensible since they allow more time for your other children. You may decide to bottlefeed, or to change to bottle-feeding quite quickly because you think that this might upset older children less, especially if they were breastfed themselves. Often there is less intimate skin-to-skin contact and less mutual touching and stroking with bottlefeeding and there is more your older children can do to help. They can fetch things, hold the bottle while one baby feeds, help with washing up, and so on. The wish to help really does need to come from your child; be patient with him and encourage him gently if he wants to do things. Remember that he has been displaced as the 'baby' of the family. Asking him to act like a grown-up and take on parental chores may make his displacement more poignant and painful. Try to be sensitive to those times he wants to act like a grown-up, and when he really wants to be a baby himself, like the twins. You can sometimes ask other people to bottlefeed so that you spend time with an older child, or ask them to play with him while you feed.

Extra attention for siblings

An older brother or sister may enjoy helping occasionally to care for their twin brothers and sisters.

Everybody notices twins and is eager to stop and admire them so their older brothers and sisters can feel really left out. To help them cope with these feelings, you could encourage grandparents or close friends to spend more time with your older children. They can make a special fuss of them, showing that they love them as much as ever. If possible, start to encourage this extra attention before the twins are born, other-wise it can seem to your children like another sign that there isn't room

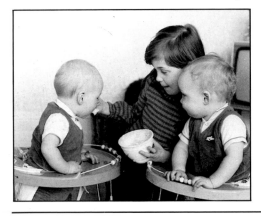

for them any more. And remind people to say hello to the older children before they rush to admire the twins. Some fathers begin to develop a closer relationship with their older children after the twins are born.

Taking siblings out

Because it's difficult to get about with twins, your other children may not find it easy to go out to see their friends. Twin prams never have seats for toddlers and are really not much help, and so if you have several small children, you may only be able to get to playgroups or nurseries if they are very close by. This may limit quite severely the extent to which your children have opportunities to make separate friends. Because of this your children – twins and others – tend to be thrown together for company.

Encouraging siblings to express their feelings

Some parents encourage their children to talk about their feelings and fantasies about their twin brothers or sisters. Children have lots of ways of expressing their anxieties and anger and you may be surprised by the things they say. Some children claim they would like to return the twins to the hospital. One young child joked about taping her twin brothers to the ceiling. Your children's feelings may also be expressed through the things they do. Cuddles can quickly turn into squeezes and pinches, and games that start as fun can get out of hand. One child, for instance, who seemed to enjoy helping her mother look after the twins expressed how angry she sometimes felt when one day she said she'd tidied them into the dustbin. If you can allow your children to talk about ideas like this without feeling too upset about it yourself, you may help them to adjust more easily. You can show them that you still love them even when they say bad things about their brothers or sisters.

GRANDPARENTS AND OTHER RELATIVES

Many mothers are pleased to have help from their families but, on the other hand, you may personally prefer to manage on your own for most of the time. But you may not have enough help, or it may be that you can't get the kind of help you want.

You may feel you can ask your own parents to help you when you don't like to ask friends and neighbours. Grandparents often enjoy help-

ing with their grandchildren; even when they have other grandchildren, they may be very thrilled to be grandparents of twins. There are a lot of things they can do. Frequently they make gifts of things like prams, washing machines, clothes or toys which reduce the cost of having twins. Often they are willing to take the twins out or give them special treats, giving the grandparents a chance to be alone with the twins and to bask in the attention that twins attract. They may also enjoy having them to stay, giving you a break and a chance to spend time with your partner or your other children. On the other hand grandparents can feel overwhelmed by the responsibility or the amount of care that two children need, and so they may prefer to take them out or have them to stay one at a time. While you may be pleased for them to have such individual attention, you may sometimes see the need to ensure that both twins are given equal chances to go out with their grandparents, and that your other children are included as well.

Some grandparents do not want to do so much; they prefer to play with their grandchildren or keep them amused only occasionally, or they may live too far away or not be fit enough to be much support on a day-to-day basis. However, they may be willing to visit you when they can, particularly if they are retired. But if they are rather frail themselves, you may feel that you need to explain to them that looking after two visitors can just add to your work, even though you do enjoy having their company.

Most grandparents are specially proud of their twin grandchildren. You may find that they are eager to help with the twins' care by taking them out or having them to stay.

MAKING COMPROMISES IN CARE

With twins the pressure to accept help is usually greater than with a single child, and you may find yourself making more compromises than you expected or than you had to with a single baby. As parents, you are the people who decide how much help you need and how you respond to the demands people make on you in return. You may find help is welcome at any price; you are willing to make compromises or to put yourself in other people's debt for a while. You may feel that you have different ideas from your parents about how you want to bring up your twins and so you are bound to clash if you are all involved in looking after them. In this case, decide which issues you think are really important and which you could give way on gracefully. For instance, you might wish to insist on dressing your twins differently, but accept your mother-in-law's choice of toys.

When relationships are strained you may not like to ask for help or you may find help difficult to accept. You may think that your relatives' help, however willingly offered, would create obligations which you would rather not fulfil. Sometimes people help in a way that makes you feel they are being critical. If this happens you could try to tell them how it appears to you and that you feel hurt. They may be more sensitive in future because they enjoy the twins' company, but if not you may prefer to go without their help.

FRIENDS AND NEIGHBOURS

You may feel happier accepting help from friends or neighbours because you are in a better position to give help in return. You may be able to leave your twins with them for half an hour while you go to the shops or they may be willing to look after an older child after school if you are delayed at the doctor or clinic. If one neighbour feels she cannot take on both twins, she might offer to have one. Local babysitters allow you to get out and do things that would be difficult with your children, such as going to the dentist or having your hair done.

Sometimes people are willing to help, but it is difficult to explain exactly what you need. For instance, friends may invite you round, without realizing just how hard it is for you to get there. Explain to them what the problems are; once people see for themselves how long everything takes and how much work toddler twins can be, they may be more understanding and more constructive in their offers of help.

TWINS CLUBS

You may find joining forces with other parents of twins a good way to get advice, support and friendship. The Twins Club can put you in touch with your local branch; you may want to consider forming one yourself if there isn't one within your neighbourhood. The Twins Club is particularly helpful if you don't have friends or relations who live nearby or if you have recently moved into the area. Even when you have lots of help you may appreciate talking to other parents who are facing problems like your own. Parents of twins sometimes babysit for one another because they have confidence in each other's ability to cope with two babies. If your children are handicapped or suffer from some specific problem you may find that other parents with similar children meet and support one another. Ask your doctor or local welfare agencies for information about self-help groups like this; they are also able to put you in touch with facilities in your area.

LOOKING AHEAD

As your twins grow older, how alike they are probably has a good deal of influence on how close they become or remain over the years, and on what kind of lives they want to lead. If you have a boy and a girl, there are many outside pressures which encourage them to grow up in separate ways, to have somewhat different interests, hopes and ideas about what they do with their lives.

For twins of the same sex, expectations don't necessarily differ in this way. How much they grow up to be separate and different depends more on their own nature and aptitudes. They may not be at all like one another, with one child academically successful and the other of a more practical nature; one musical, the other tone deaf; one intuitive, the other logical. It helps if you are not too anxious about their differing types and levels of achievement, but appreciate each child for what he or she is. Young twins can find it a heavy burden if people expect them to do as well as one another all the time. The burden can become heavier as they get older and have very public events like school reports or exam results that measure their abilities. Being compared with a twin all the time can be hurtful and destructive, and might even make them less ready to work at school.

TEENAGE TWINS

While your twins are young, you have a lot of control over things like how they are dressed and have their hair cut. As they get older they probably want to decide these things for themselves. For instance, if you have always dressed them differently in the early days, they may later decide to make the most of being twins and start to dress alike. But you can feel reassured that they are acting by choice and not because they are emotionally unable to be different. Adolescence is a time when boys and girls experiment with all sorts of roles and belong to different groups, trying each out for size. Being twinny may be just one more experiment they want to try. Probably the less you show disapproval or argue with them, the more quickly they are likely to get through such phases. Going to parties dressed identically, confusing people or playing tricks can be fun for them. Being a twin has its problems, but it is good to bear in mind that it is also something your children can enjoy.

BECOMING INDEPENDENT

All children have to face the task of separating from their parents and families, and of learning to become independent. Twins may also have to separate from each other, and cope with each other's growing independence. Identical twins may find this hardest. You may have read about or even seen adult twins who still dress alike or live together and who are very happy to remain close. Once twins have experienced a very close relationship with each other, they may find it harder to be alone or to make the effort to get to know new people. Making friends is a slow process; if they don't have opportunities for this when they are young it may be a struggle for them later, which is why we have talked a lot about separation and becoming independent in this book. We believe that the lives of twins are richer and more satisfying if they are given opportunities to cope alone as well as together. In this way we hope they can choose more freely whether or when they want to be alone, with their twin or to be close to other people.

SPECIAL CASES

OLDER MOTHERS

If you are an older mother (usually that means if you are over 35), you are more carefully checked during your pregnancy. You may be given an ultrasound scan even when they are not given routinely to younger women at your hospital and you may be offered a bloodtest (alphafeto-protein or AFP) to check your babies' health. If you have been given ovulation-inducing drugs you may be scanned specifically to check whether you are pregnant with twins. With ultrasound scanning you may discover quite early in your pregnancy that you are expecting twins.

Amniocentesis

Because there is a slightly higher risk of chromosomal abnormalities in babies born to older mothers, you may be offered amniocentesis, if the facilities are available in your hospital. By testing some of the fluid in the babies' amniotic sacs, it is possible to learn whether either of your babies will be born with conditions such as spina bifida or Down's syndrome (mongolism).

In an amniocentesis, a small sample of the amniotic fluid is removed painlessly from your uterus when you are about sixteen weeks pregnant. The fluid is analysed so that two to four weeks later the hospital can give you the result, which usually indicates that your babies are fine and you can continue your pregnancy without worry. As with any procedure, there are slight risks with amniocentesis; there is a small chance of mis-carrying, but to minimize the chances of this happening you are given an ultrasound scan first, so the medical staff have a clear idea of where the placenta is lying before inserting the needle to draw out the fluid.

It can be difficult to decide whether to have an amniocentesis if you are offered one, especially when you know you are expecting twins. On the one hand it is reassuring to know that the test has found nothing wrong. On the other hand you have the anxiety of deciding whether to terminate your pregnancy if the test indicates there is something wrong. Unfortunately the timing of the test means you have to make up your mind quickly, since your pregnancy is quite advanced by the time the results come through.

If you learn that both your twins are handicapped you have a harsh and difficult choice to face. You have to think about the severity and the nature of the handicap and about how well you can cope with and bring up two such handicapped children. When the test indicates that there is something wrong with only one of your babies you have an even more cruel decision to make; you have to decide whether you can come to terms with having a handicapped child in order to give birth to the one who is healthy. You may be among the many couples who feel that they want to decline the test, preferring to face reality when it comes at birth.

HANDICAPPED
TWINS

Having a handicapped child is always a shock to parents. It can shatter their self-confidence and can make them blame themselves; what did they do wrong; what more could they have done. Having a handicapped child can seem like a punishment, making parents look for things they have done to deserve their unhappiness.

There are many different kinds of handicap; some come about because of something unusual with the twins' genes and chromosomes (such as Down's syndrome). If your twins are identical, when one is handicapped in this way, the other is likely to be. If they are non-identical, one or both of them may be handicapped. Other sorts of handicap happen because something goes wrong in early pregnancy or at birth. For instance, deafness can be caused by German measles (rubella) in the early weeks of pregnancy and cerebral palsy by lack of oxygen during labour or following birth. These types of handicap can affect one or both twins, regardless of whether they are identical or not.

Like many parents, you may reject your handicapped babies at first. When you cannot hold or feed them it may take longer to come to love them. When they need surgery you may hold back your feelings because of your fears for your babies' lives. They may take a long time to get to know you, to look at you and smile when you come near. Once they recognize you and respond to you, you may find it easier to realize that they are yours and to accept them.

Coming to terms with handicap

Later you may come to see that your children are in many respects just like any others. You grow to love them for themselves and make the necessary adjustments to your lives so you can take care of them. This takes a long time for some people: quite how long depends on things like the sort of handicap your child suffers and its severity. If just one of your twins is handicapped, you'll have many sadly conflicting feelings to deal with. You might find it easier to build up a loving relationship with the child who is not handicapped, but alternatively you may find yourself taken up with caring for the one who is. Either way you both probably have to cope with feelings of guilt and sadness. Sharing your love and attention equally between your twins may seem impossible in the circumstances.

With handicapped twins, you need help, so do ask to see the social worker at the hospital. There are organizations you can contact for support and advice. Many of these are run by parents in your situation and others are run by charities or by local welfare services. Their addresses are given at the end of this section.

WHEN BABIES DIE

Although today very tiny and sickly babies are much more likely to live than in the past, some babies do still die. If your babies die before birth or during labour they are stillborn; the deaths of babies in the first month of life are known as neonatal deaths; perinatal death is a combination of stillbirth and death in the first week of life.

A sick baby is usually taken to the special care baby unit (see page 43); there is little you can do at this time but watch and wait. Most babies survive and eventually go home, but while they are in the unit sometimes you may feel that it is too painful to look at, touch or care for them if they are so ill that you are afraid they may die. Because you love your babies you may feel too anguished to show it by getting involved with their care. Your anxiety may lead you to seek more reassurances than the medical staff can give, or to feel angry that not enough is being done. It helps if medical staff and your own family understand why you are acting in this way and respect your feelings.

Your babies' deaths may come as a relief if it has been touch and go for some time and they have shown no signs of improvement. You may feel it is better to know the worst than to go on and on being kept in uncertainty. However sad their deaths, and whenever they occur, you may feel that once they have happened you can start to grieve. Hospitals are now much more concerned to encourage parents to see and hold their babies when they die. Some offer you a photograph of your babies, and you yourselves may like to photograph them too. It makes their existence more real to you and you may feel reassured by their appearance.

Hospitals also encourage you to name your babies. Your loss is of babies you were only just beginning to know from the way they moved around inside you or from the brief time you were together after they were born. You don't have the great storehouse of memories that you do when someone older dies, but you can try to build up a picture of your babies to mourn now and to remember later. Hospitals are usually willing to organize your babies' funerals, but you can do this yourselves if you prefer. If you don't attend the funeral you may still wish to ask the hospital to be sure to tell you what has been done with your babies' remains.

WHEN ONE TWIN SURVIVES

When one twin dies but the other lives, your feelings will be a desperate contradiction; loss and grief for the twin who has died and relief and joy that the other twin is doing well. You probably feel very confused. Unlike parents who have lost a single baby or both twins, you cannot give yourselves over to grief completely; you still have a living baby to look after. You may feel that you should not be happy or enjoy your surviving baby knowing that her twin is dead. But at the same time you know she needs you to love her and be happy to have her.

Because few people can understand what you are going through, the things they say and do can leave you even more muddled. They may pretend it hasn't happened or act as though you shouldn't grieve because you still have one healthy baby. Torn and guilty yourself, you too may try to blot out your feelings for your dead baby. Even when other people want to help, they may find it hard to know when you want to talk about your pain and grief; sometimes you'll want to talk about your dead baby as well as about thinking ahead to your life with the surviving baby. Try to express yourself to someone close and sympathetic; you may like to ask your doctor to arrange for you to talk to someone to help you come to terms with your confused emotions.

DEATH AND THE FAMILY

Your whole family may experience grief and pain at losing the babies. Your parents have been looking forward to being grandparents and your other children may have been anticipating their new brothers and sisters. Children can have odd ideas about death and may not express their feelings in the same way as adults. The way they ask questions may come about because they do not know how to talk about someone who has died. When they ask questions like, When are the babies coming back? or What did they look like when they were dead?, they don't realize they might be hurting you.

Children may also behave unlike their usual selves because they need reassurance and love. They may imagine that the dead baby has been kidnapped or stolen and may fear it could happen to them, so you might find they suddenly start having nightmares or are afraid of the dark. If you are both too upset yourselves to comfort them at first, ask other people like friends or grandparents to take extra care of them.

You may not feel able to cope with your own feelings, let alone with those of the people close to you. But even when you're feeling low, you have still got a lot to give your partner and your family. They may try to help you with your grief by encouraging you to get out or to celebrate a birthday. This may upset you if it seems to you that they are not respecting your babies' death. Even though you probably appreciate their attempts to help you, you may sometimes resent them for trying to make you act as if you were happy.

LIVING WITH GRIEF

You may grieve for a long time after the loss of your babies; longer than you might expect. Some mothers say they still feel sad years afterwards; when even then things will bring back memories. Anniversaries of your babies' birth or death can be a difficult time. You may find it hard to explain to other people that you do want to remember your babies even though it brings back the tears and pain. You may both gain strength by sharing your grief with each other, your family or friends. And if you are allowed to grieve and mourn you will be better able, eventually, to accept your babies' death. You may be helped, too, by talking to other bereaved parents. There are a number of groups which help one another in this way; their addresses are given below.

Antenatal and postnatal support
National Childbirth Trust, Alexandra House,
Oldham Terrace, London W3
0181 992 8637

Breast Feeding Support Groups
The National Childbirth Trust - See above

La Leche League
BM 3424, London WC1N 3XX
0171 242 1278

Children in Hospital
National Association for the Welfare of Children
in Hospital
Argyle House, Euston Rd, London NW1
0171-833-2041

National Association for The Education of Sick
Children
17 Old Ford Rd, London E2
0181 980 8523

Contraceptive Advice
The Family Planning Association
2 Pentonville Rd, London N1
0171 837 4044 (Helpline), 0171 837 5432
(Switchboard)

Counselling
Relate Marriage Guidance
National Headquarters, Herbert Gray College,
Little Church Street, Rugby
01788 573241

Handicapped Children
Downs Syndrome Association
153 Mitcham Rd, London SW17
0181 682 4001

Association for Spina Bifida and Hydrocephalus
Asbah House, 42 Park Road, Peterborough PE1
2UQ
01733 5559888

MENCAP
123 Golden Lane, LondonEC1
0171 454 0454

Local Playgroups, etc.
Pre-school Learning Alliance
National Centre, 61 Kings Cross Rd, London
WC1
National Centre Helpline - 0171 837 5513

Pre-school Playgroups Association
Sub-Committee Branch Offices, Linden House,
Rectory Rd, London N16

One Parent Families
National Council for One Parent Families
255 Kentish Town Rd, London NW5 7LX

Gingerbread Association for One Parent Families
16-17 Clerkenwell Close, London EC1 70AA

Stillbirth
Stillbirth and Neonatal Death Society (SANDS)
28 Portland Place, London W1
0171 436 5881 (Helpline) 0171 436 7940
(Admin/Publications)

Samaritans 0345 909090
for deaf callers, 0181 780 2521

Twins and Twins Clubs
Twins and Multiple Births Association (TAMBA)
PO Box 30, Little Sutton, South Wirral, L66 1TH
0151 348 0020

Australian NHMRC Twin Registry
Dr John Hopper, c/o The University of
Melbourne, 200 Berkeley St, Carlton, Victoria
3053, Australia

AMBA Inc
PO Box 105, Coogee 2034, NSW, Australia

New Zealand Multiple Births Association
PO Box 1258, Wellington, New Zealand

Parent Care
PO Box 8297, Symonds Street, Auckland, New
Zealand

Chapter 1
MacGillivray, I., Nylander, P. P. S. and Corney, G. *Human Multiple Reproduction,* W. B. Saunders Co. Ltd 1975, London, Phildelphia, Toronto.
Pfeffer, N. and Woollett, A. *The Experience of Infertility,* Virago, London, 1983.
Mittler, P. *The Study of Twins,* Penguin, Harmondsworth, 1971.
Wileman, A. in Stephanie Dowrick and Sibyl Grandberg (eds) *Why Children?* The Women's Press, London, 1980.

Chapters 2 and 3
Kitzinger, S. *Pregnancy and Childbirth,* Michael Joseph, 1980.
Beels, C. *The Childbirth Book,* Turnstone Books, London, 1978.
Dale, B. and Roeber, J. *Exercises for Childbirth,* Century Publishing Co., London 1982.
Macfarlane, A. *The Psychology of Childbirth,* Fontana, London 1977.
Klaus, R. A. and Kennell, J. H. *Maternal-Infant Bonding,* C. V. Mosby, St. Louis.
Breen, D. *Talking with Mothers; About Pregnancy, Childbirth and Early Motherhood,* Jill Norman and Hobhouse, London 1981.
Oakley, A. *From Here to Maternity: Becoming a Mother,* Penguin, Harmondsworth, 1981.

Chapters 4 and 5
Leach, P. *Babyhood,* Penguin, Harmondsworth, 2nd edition 1983.
Dunn, J. *Distress and Comfort,* Fontana, London 1977.
Newson, J. and Newson, E. *Patterns of Infant Care in an Urban Community,* Penguin, Harmondsworth, 1963.
Jolly, H. *More Commonsense About Babies and Children,* Sphere 1978.
Messenger, M. *The Breastfeeding Book,* Century Publishing Co., London 1982.
Kitzinger, S. *The Experience of Breastfeeding,* Penguin, Harmondsworth, 1979.
Phillips, A. and Rakusen, J. *Our Bodies Ourselves,* British Edition: Penguin, Harmondsworth 1978.
Martin, J. and Monk, J. *Infant Feeding,* O.P.C.S. Social Survey Division London 1980.

Chapter 6
Lytton, H. *Parent-Child Interaction; The Socialization Process Observed in Twin and Singleton Families,* Plenum Press, New York 1980.
Svenka Savic. *How Twins Learn to Talk; A Study of the Speech Development of Twins from 1-3,* Academic Press, London, 1980.
Luria, A. R. and Yudovitch, F. Ia. *Speech and the Development of Mental Processes in the Child,* Penguin, Harmondsworth, 1978.
Friedman, S. L. and Sigman, M. (eds) *Preterm Birth and Psychological Development,* Academic Press, New York 1981.

De Villiers, P. A. and De Villiers, J. G. *Early Language,* Fontana, London, 1979.
Snow, C. E. and Ferguson, C. A. (eds) *Talking to Children; Language Input and Acquisition,* Cambridge University Press, Cambridge 1977.
Newson, J. J. and Newson, E. *Four Years Old in an Urban Community,* Penguin, Harmondsworth 1968.
Butler, D. *Babies Need Books,* Penguin, Harmondsworth, 1980.
Garvey, C. *Play,* Fontana, London 1977.
Rubin, Z. *Children's Friendships,* Fontana, London 1980.
Dunn, J. and Kendrick, C. *Siblings; Love, Envy and Understanding,* Grant McIntyre, London 1982.
Lewis, M. and Rosenblum, L. A. (eds) *Interaction, Conversation and the Development of Language,* Wiley, New York 1977.

Chapter 7
Clulow, C. F. *To Have and To Hold; Marriage, The first Baby and Preparing Couples for Parenthood,* Aberdeen University Press, Aberdeen, 1982.
Beail, N. and McGuire, J. (eds) *Fathers; Psychological Perspectives,* Junction Books, London 1982.
Oakley, A. *From Here to Maternity: Becoming a Mother,* Penguin, Harmondsworth, 1981.
McKee, L. and O'Brien, M. (eds) *The Father Figure,* Tavistock, London 1982.
Dunn, J. and Kendrick, C. *Siblings: Love, Envy and Understanding,* Grant McIntyre, London 1982.
Rapoport, R., Rapoport, R. N. and Strelitz, Z. *Fathers, Mothers and Others,* Routledge and Kegan Paul, London, 1977.
Mittler, P. *The Study of Twins,* Penguin, Harmondsworth 1971.
Baker, D. *Cassandra at the Wedding,* Virago Modern Classics, London 1982.
Friedman, S. L. and Sigman, M. (eds) *Preterm Birth and Psychological Development,* Academic Press, New York 1981.

Special Cases
Pfeffer, N. and Woollett, A. *The Experience of Infertility,* Virago, London, 1983.
Borg, S. and Lasker, J. *When Pregnancy Fails: Families Coping With Miscarriage, Stillbirth and Infant Death,* Beacon Press 1981.
Campling, J. (ed) *Images of Ourselves: Women with Disabilities Talking,* Routledge and Kegan Paul, London 1981.
Hannam, C. *Parents and Mentally Handicapped Children,* Penguin, Harmondsworth Second edition 1980.
Kubler-Ross, E. *On Death and Dying,* Macmillan, 1970.
Parkes, C. M. *Bereavement: Studies of Grief in Adult Life,* Penguin, Harmondsworth, 1975.

Authors' acknowledgements

Many people have helped to make this book – and, in particular, Averil's study of twin families – possible. We cannot name them all, but would like to thank the people listed below. Although they all gave us assistance and support, the responsibility for the ideas and information in the book is entirely ours.

We are grateful to Dr. David Harvey, Dr. Elizabeth Bryan and Professor Elder of the Queen Charlotte's and Hammersmith Hospitals. Interviews with families often took place in the clinics and wards of Queen Charlotte's and the Hammersmith. The obstetric, paediatric, nursing and other staff were always welcoming. The ultrasound staff at both hospitals kept records of twin pregnancies so that Averil could contact families. The reception staff at the antenatal clinics of both hospitals were always efficient, and cheerfully assisted her in finding records and getting to know the hospital routines and procedures. Because the majority of the families came from Queen Charlotte's Hospital the demands made on the staff there were particularly heavy. Averil would also like to thank Eve Vinten for the many and valued ways in which she helped. The Medical Committee and members of the Twins Club association generously shared their ideas about twins and their families.

Dr. David White, Denis Gahagan, Brian Clifford, Louise Lyon, Anita Colloms and Maire Messenger of the Psychology Department, North East London Polytechnic have all given support in many ways. Mary Towers and Anne Barritt typed the manuscript. Sheila Kitzinger of the NCT was enthusiastic and encouraging when the study was still in its infancy. Cherry Rowland also shared and discussed ideas. Our families, Paul and Steve, Catherine, Thomas, Roger and Christopher have all put up cheerfully with our preoccupation with writing about twins.

Most of all we are grateful to the families who took part in the study. They shared their experiences willingly and gave time and energy repeatedly when they were already busy and tired, and they allowed themselves and their children to be watched and observed. We owe this book to their generosity, and we hope that they will find we have echoed truthfully the broad and varied nature of their thoughts about their twins.

Publishers Acknowledgements

The publishers would like to thank the following families for allowing themselves to be photographed for this book: the Cobachas, the Collinges, the Davises, the Edges, the Elwells, the Hansons, the Hardcastles, the Hiltons, the Kirdwoods, the Lindsays, the Mansours, the Matthews, the Lloyds, the Oakhams, the O'Boyles, the Oldfields and the Rowlands. Special thanks also for help from Gillian Liddiard and the Tooting Twins Club, and to the staff of St. Mary's Hospital, Paddington.

Editor: Nicky Adamson
Art Editor: Roger Walton
Editorial liaison: Sarah Mitchell

Art Director: Debbie MacKinnon

Photographs by Nancy Durrell McKenna
Anatomical illustrations by Elaine Keenan
Figure illustrations by Jenny Powell
Equipment illustrations by Jim Robbins
Photographic prints by Adrian Ensor
Retouching by Nick Oxtoby

Filmset by Chambers Wallace Ltd.,
Unit 8, 3 Long Street, London E2
